MW01630513

The Metalsmith's Book of

BOXES & LOCKETS

Also by Tim McCreight
Jewelry: Fundamentals of Metalsmithing

Other titles in this series
Baskets: A Book for Makers & Collectors
Billie Ruth Sudduth

Etched Glass: Techniques & Designs
Norm and Ruth Dobbins

Needle Lace: Techniques & Inspiration
Jill Nordfors Clark

The Metalsmith's Book of

BOXES & LOCKETS

Tim McCreight

THE METALSMITH'S BOOK OF BOXES & LOCKETS
By Tim McCreight

Photographer (studio demonstrations): Robert Diamante
Design: Jane Tenenbaum
Editor: Katie Kazan
Editorial Assistants: Robert Winters; Nikki Muenchow

Published by Brynmorgen Press, Portland, Maine
www.Brynmorgen.com

This book was originally published by
The Guild and Hand Books Press under ISBN 0-9658248-9-6.

Printed in China

ISBN 1-929565-23-2

Front cover artwork. Top, left to right: Kiff Slemmons, *Metabox,* box with rings, silver, ebony, pencil, ruler, photo: Rod Slemmons; making a dome, photo: Robert Diamante; Lori Talcott, *Baby Virginia Turns 80,* sterling, pebble, 25"L, photo: Richard Nicol (this piece is also shown on the title page). Center: Jan Baum, *Varying Direction #2,* pendant/locket. Bottom, left to right: Carol Webb, *Willie's Box,* photo-etched copper over fine silver; making a basic hinge, photo: Robert Diamante; Deborah Krupenia, *Tagasode II (Whose Sleeves?),* colored golds, sterling, Japanese copper alloys, photo: Dean Powell.

Other artwork. Page 2, Nicole DesChamps, *My Family Reliquary,* sterling, brass, aluminum, found objects, photos. Title page: Lori Talcott, *Baby Virginia Turns 80* (see description above). Back cover: Stephen Yusko, *Gift Box,* steel, 4 1/4"H x 6 1/4"W x 3 3/4"D, photo: Robert O'Neil.

Contents

Patty Bolz, container pendant. 22K, boulder opal, sapphire, diamonds, 2 1/4"H, photo: Robert Diamante.

Introduction

What is it about boxes that draws us to them so irresistibly? We might admire a candlestick simply by looking, but we're compelled to pick up a box or locket and open it. Perhaps it's the toy-like action of a catch and hinge, or the mystery of wondering what might be inside. Perhaps our fascination comes in part from other experiences of boxes: a universal memory of childhood treasures in shoe boxes and tobacco tins.

Marjorie Simon, *Triangular Dancing Boxes.* Brass, wood, paint, resin, 4"H x 4"W x 4"D, photo: Bobby Hansson. These boxes were excercises in scoring and folding. They were made from 12" squares of 20-gauge brass. The legs are painted wooden caning pegs, and the colored elements are epoxy resin on brass.

In 1997, I wrote a book called *Jewelry: Fundamentals of Metalsmithing,* a book that described the basic techniques common to almost all jewelry education. The skills that follow "basics" are usually termed "intermediate," but that term is, at best, ambiguous. It describes a zone neither basic nor advanced—an array of widely varying procedures and techniques.

The Metalsmith's Book of Boxes and Lockets explains a number of these more-than-basic techniques through the device of box making, with the topic divided into its constituent parts: box, hinge and catch. This allows for a creative mix-and-match—think of children's books that are slit to allow each page to be a reconfigured creature. Select a box technique, match it with a hinge, then choose a catch to complete the piece. In this way, I've tried to create a structure that is clear without being narrow. This is followed by a section called "Basics and Practices" that provides instruction in soldering, tube making, and other general topics that apply to making boxes and lockets. The appendix includes useful reference data and a list of suppliers.

Lockets and boxes offer a wonderful format for metalsmiths. Technically, they call upon a set of skills that can challenge anyone: hinges that slide fluidly, seams that disappear, catches that click with confident assurance. Mastery of these construction techniques is not only a reward in itself, but a valuable aid in other metalworking activities. The ability to make a neat hinge will, for example, translate into improved technique in measuring, soldering and fitting—all important skills for stonesetting, surface decoration and other activities.

So, take a hinge from here and a catch from there, and while you're at it, make up your own variations. Season this information with the exciting finished work shown here, and synthesize these ingredients into objects that are as satisfying to use as they are to make.

Metalworking Safety

Safety in metalworking depends on adhering to the following principles:

- Common sense
- Knowledge and respect for the machines
- Common sense
- Avoiding dangerous materials and processes
- Common sense
- Protecting yourself from invasion by particles, fumes or sharp objects

Because everyone's body is unique, even officially tolerable levels of a material may be intolerable for you. Pay attention to the early signs your body sends: if you have a dry mouth, an odd taste, a rash, nausea or dizziness, stop what you're doing and take a break. Systematically eliminate procedures in order to identify the source of the problem. As a creative person, you will then be able to come up with an alternate approach.

Any time you work near a motor-driven tool, there is a danger of getting snagged. Always keep hair and clothing tied back out of the way when drilling, buffing and grinding. *Always wear goggles.* When grinding or buffing with a machine, be certain the dust is directed away from you, and use a respirator if working for more than a minute. Be especially careful to avoid breathing toxic materials like bone, antler, metallic gem material (e.g., malachite) and exotic woods.

Kristina Kada, *A Core of Gold*, locket. Fine silver, 18K, 1"Dia, photo: Ralph Gabriner.

Minimize the use of strong solvents when possible. Label all chemicals and store them in a safe place in an appropriate container. Wear rubber gloves, splash-proof goggles and an apron.

Fire is an integral part of metalworking, and a good metalsmith is comfortable with flame. But comfortable doesn't mean careless. Always use the "soapy water test" when refitting a regulator or tank, and replace the tank if there is any problem. Turn off the tanks and drain hoses at the end of the day. Sniff the air when you enter the studio; exit immediately if you smell gas.

Never set combustibles, like paper towels or drawings, on the soldering table, and always quench charcoal blocks when leaving the studio. Wear dark glasses for prolonged soldering, or if your eyes are getting sore.

Repeated actions, such as hammering, can trigger carpal tunnel syndrome and similar disorders. Get in the habit of "shaking out" your hands every ten minutes and stop work immediately if your fingers are numb or tingly. It is often possible to adjust positions and angles to correct these problems.

Talya Baharal, *Tool Box.* Sterling.

1

Building a Box

This chapter describes several techniques used to make the "body" of a box or locket. Along the way it introduces some useful tools. For more complete information about basic studio procedures, see Chapter 4, "Basics and Practices."

Making a Rectangular Box

A simple rectangular box is both basic and elegant. Its crisp corners, straightforward form and versatile shape make it a box format you'll use often. Simple variations on the proportions will yield everything from a treasure chest to a locket on a charm bracelet.

Layout

The selection of metal and thickness will depend on the use of the piece and the value you want to attach to it. The techniques described here apply equally to gold, sterling, brass, nickel silver and copper. Any may be used, though gold and sterling will, of course, result in a more valuable piece. Base metals will tarnish more quickly, but they can be finished with patinas that have a beauty all their own. Because the process is almost identical regardless of the metal being used, it's possible—in fact,

Mark Stanitz, box. Sterling, 5"H x 3"W x 3"D.

wise—to test a design in an inexpensive metal before undertaking a final piece in silver or gold. This is more than a matter of simple caution and frugality. When materials are inexpensive, you may be more willing to take risks with both design and technique. And how does anyone learn except by taking risks?

The example shown is 2" wide by 1" deep and 3/4" high (5 cm x 2.5 cm x 2 cm). I've used 22-gauge sterling, though the slightly thicker 20-gauge would also be a good choice. A gauge heavier than these would increase the cost, make the process more difficult, and yield a box I'd consider bulky. I'd advise against using thinner material (like 24-gauge), because it's likely to warp during soldering. Also remember that after all construction is completed you'll need to file, sand and polish the box. Each of these processes removes material, so it's smart to start with stock a little thicker than the desired result.

Make one edge of a sheet perfectly straight by filing with a flat file. Check the edge by holding it up to the light against a ruler or other reliable straightedge. The metal may have come from the supplier with a good edge, but always check to be sure. This edge will be the baseline for all other measurements, so don't move on until it's perfect.

Use a *machinist's square* (also called a *try square*) to scribe two lines exactly perpendicular to the first edge. Note that the $5 carpenter's square used for cutting lumber is not exact enough for work on this scale. Invest in a precise square and treat it with respect.

The easiest way to scribe a line parallel to the edge is also the most reliable. Open a pair of dividers to the total height of the box (including the height of the lid), set one leg just over the edge, and pull the tool along the metal. This will leave a delicate scratched line. Now determine the height of the box *without* the lid, and scribe this line in the same way.

Using a ruler, measure off a panel slightly larger than two adjacent sides: the front and one side, for instance. These measurements can be rough and will be made more exact later. Cut two identical pieces, so you'll have a front-and-a-side and a back-and-a-side.

Talya Baharal, *Ball House*, object. Sterling, 14K, copper, brass, 5 1/2"H x 2"W x 1 1/4"D, photo: Gene Grida.

To lay out a strip with parallel sides, drag one leg of a dividers along a prepared edge. Scrub the metal with Scotch-Brite in a circular motion so the scratch line shows clearly.

Kiff Slemmons, *Overruled*.
Sterling, ebony, ruler,
2½"H x 4½"W x 1½"D,
photos: Rod Slemmons.
The silver handle swings down to allow removal of the 13 rings. This piece plays with our instant recognition of familiar shapes and materials, spinning them into humorous juxtapositions.

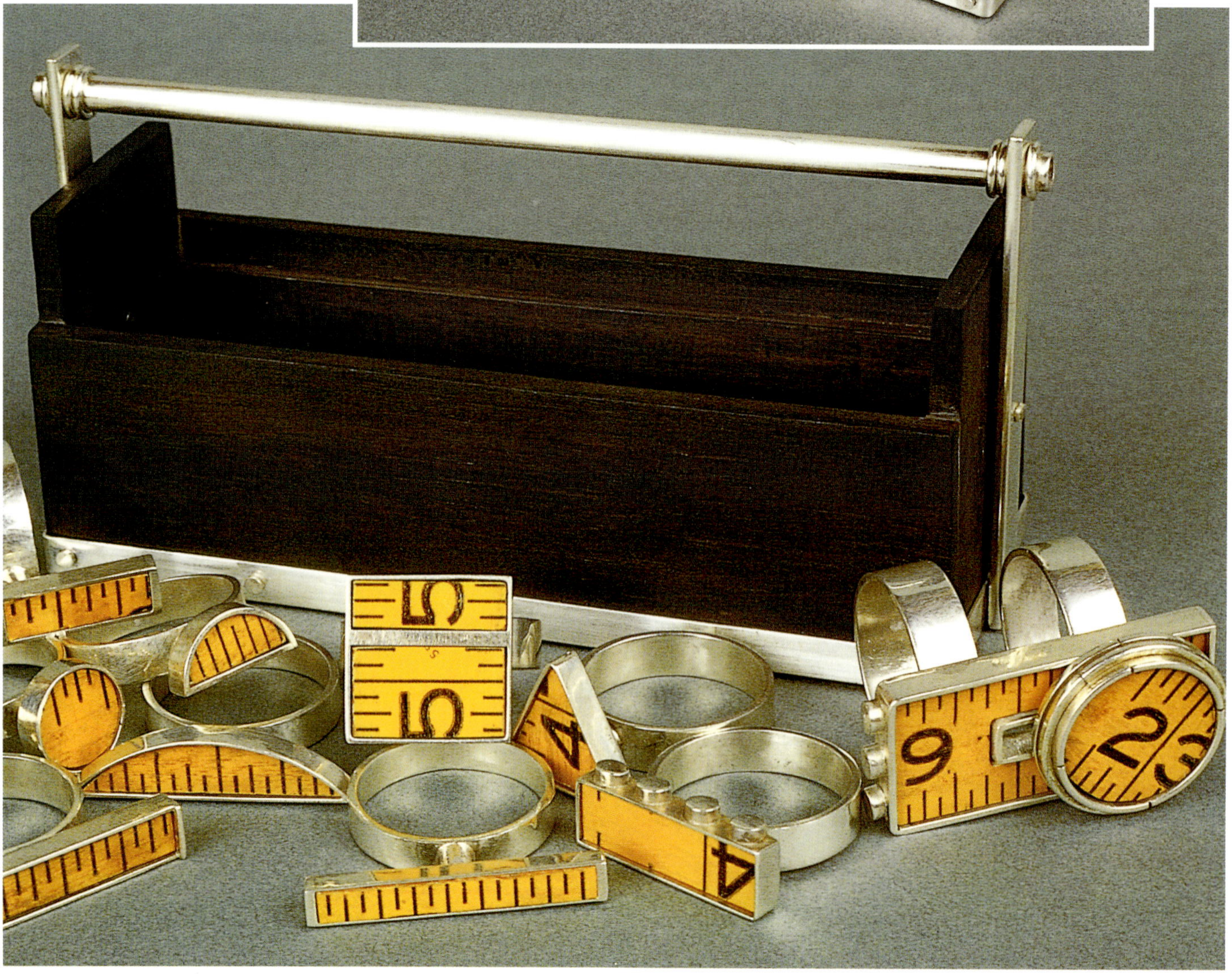

In its simplest form (and without a top) a box has five panels: front, side, back, side and bottom. Metalsmiths don't usually assemble a box from five separate pieces, however, because of the difficulty in keeping them properly aligned. It's much more common to measure, cut and then bend pieces of sheet metal large enough to accommodate two or three of the panels at once.

Bending Corners

The bending process has a huge effect on the appearance of the box or locket. Corners can be crisp or rounded, precise or approximate, square or irregular. As much as any other element in box making, this sets the tone of the box.

There are many ways to bend a sheet of metal, and each option has its appropriate uses. Let's examine them in a sequence that runs from rounded to crisp corners.

Tim McCreight, box. Sterling, 1/2"H x 2 1/2"W x 1 1/2"D.

BENDING CORNERS

1 Use a square to establish the corner, checking it from both sides to be certain the angle is correct.

2 A bending brake can be used to make corners without scoring. Brakes come in all sizes, from a simple model like this to huge, motor-driven units.

The easiest way to bend sheet metal is to press it over a sharp edge, like the edge of a tabletop. Depending on the thickness and malleability of the metal, this can give a relatively sharp corner. A slightly crisper corner can be made by grasping the metal between two pieces of hardwood or similar supports in a sturdy vise, and then bending it by tapping with a plastic or leather mallet.

John J. Grant, *Pin Hole Bolo*. Steel, photographs, found objects.

Bending Brake

A tool called a *bending brake* is designed with the sole function of bending a neat corner. Brakes are made of metal and range in size from two-foot tabletop models to enormous units as large as a truck. They all have a horizontal metal table or bed, and a gripping plate that holds a piece of sheet metal in place. A hinged arm lifts the metal, either by hand or with hydraulics, to bend it.

To see corners made this way, just look around. Toasters and refrigerators are metal boxes made in brakes, as are filing cabinets, truck bodies and desks. Brakes made for small-scale work are not terribly expensive; they're a reasonable investment when many bends are needed.

Scoring

To bend a really crisp corner in sheet or wire, it's necessary to create a groove along the fold line. The idea is to cut a V-groove that will translate to a mitered corner when the adjacent panels are bent together in such a way that the groove is closed. The angle of the V determines the angle of the corner (or vice-versa). To create a square corner, the angle of each side must be 45°, which is to say, the V must have a 90° angle. An easy formula to obtain the angle of the corner is to subtract the angle of the V from 180°.

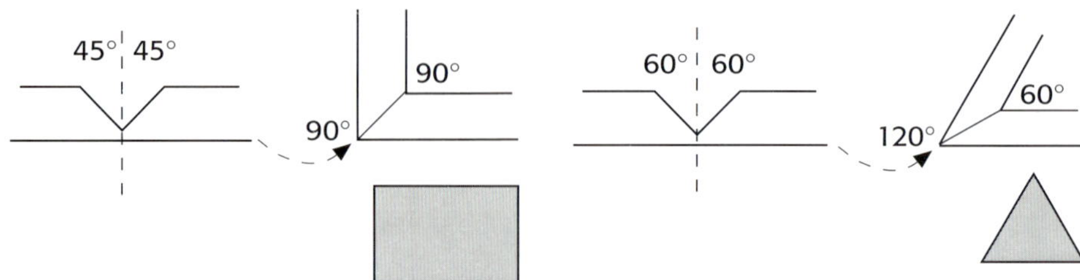

Corners are made by filing a V-groove; the angles of the V are determined by the corner you want to create. For a square corner, remove 45° from each side of a centerline so the resulting groove has a 90° angle. A triangular box calls for wide V's with interior angles of 120°.

Five Techniques for Making a Groove

Grooves can be made in several ways, from quick-and-rough to painstaking-and-accurate. Typically, the choice of method depends on the length of the bend, the tools at hand, and personal preference.

1. Hammering Against a Corner

This is a quick method often used by blacksmiths to create a V-groove. Select a sharp corner, typically on an anvil or, as shown, on a bench block. Hold the sheet at a 45° angle and strike a confident blow onto the sheet at the same angle. The hammer face should hit the metal flat on. It's best if this is done in a single blow, because with each strike the metal risks shifting.

Because the blow will have severely work-hardened the metal at exactly the point where we need it to bend, the corner must now be annealed. The groove is then refined with a file and bent. Solder is melted along the groove to strengthen the corner.

Micki Lippe, *Spirit Box*. Sterling, 22K, nickel silver, 3/4"H x 3"W x 3"D, photo: Richard Nicol. Fabricated from sheets of metal with a casual confidence, the pierced square hole in the center invites us in, then immediately stops us with a golden barricade. The rich color on the nickel silver is achieved by warming the piece with a soft torch flame.

2. Using a Wire

In this variation on the method just described, a tough wire is substituted for the anvil corner. Lay a piece of steel wire (piano wire, paper clip, etc.) across the sheet where you want the bend to occur. Use tape to hold it in place or bend it in such a way that it grips the sheet. Strike the wire with a hammer, and again try to impress the entire groove in a single blow. Do not use a hammer with a polished face, because the wire may scar it. As before, anneal the sheet before attempting to bend it.

A variation on this technique uses a rolling mill to press the wire into the sheet. This method is a little difficult to control because the

MAKING A GROOVE

1 The fastest way to create a groove is to strike the annealed sheet over a sharp edge. The metal must be annealed again before trying to make the bend.

2 A hardened steel wire is struck with a hammer to press a crease into the metal for folding. Here again, it's important to anneal the sheet before bending.

3 A separating disk, here used with a flexible shaft machine, is used to cut away material for a folding groove. Goggles must be worn when grinding like this.

wire is out of sight between the rollers at the moment it's doing its job. The advantage of using the mill—the tremendous pressure it creates—is offset by the tendency of this pressure to magnify minor irregularities. If a wire is even slightly curved, the groove it creates will probably be very curved. This makes the technique effective for organically shaped boxes, but not for precise angles.

3. Grinding

This technique uses a *separating disk*, a wafer-thin wheel of silicon carbide abrasive, in a flexible shaft machine to cut a groove. The trench that results has vertical walls; to angle the walls outward, run the corner of a square needle file along the groove. It's particularly important to protect your eyes with goggles whenever you use a flexible shaft machine.

4. Scraping

The preceding methods are difficult to control for sheets over a

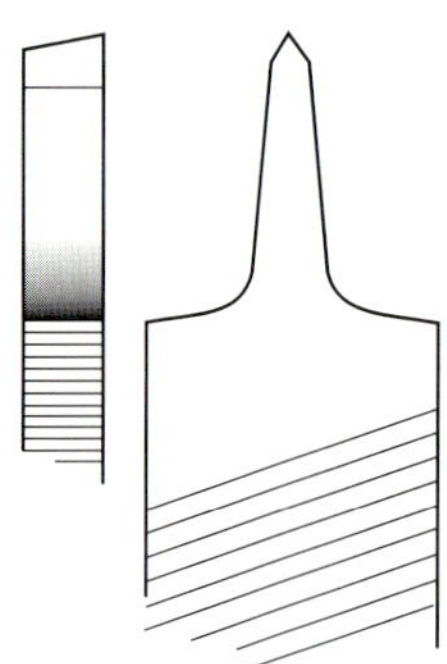

couple of inches. Scraping is a more effective alternative for these cases.

In this process, a hardened steel tool is dragged across a surface to scrape off flakes of metal. If possible, clamp the sheet onto the table as shown, using cardboard pads at the clamps to avoid scarring the metal. Because the area below the end of the scored groove can become damaged, place a piece of scrap wood or matte board under the metal sheet to protect the table. Use a scribe and straightedge to start the line, making a dozen or so passes, then continue with a scraper, increasing the pressure as the groove gets deeper.

To make a scraper from a file, grind or file a point on the tip of the tang. It will look like the roof of a very tiny house and should slope toward one end. The angle of the "roof" will determine the shape of the scored V.

Arrange a torch so you can have both hands free while heating the tool. With a stout pair of pliers in one hand and the file in the other, heat the last 1/2" of the tang to a bright red color. Moving quickly, grasp the tip and bend as shown. If the tip isn't bent far enough, return the tool to the flame and repeat the process. When you have the angle right, heat the tip to bright red again and quench it immediately in water. This simplified approach to hardening is sufficient for this tool. Use sandpaper or a whetstone to hone the tip if necessary; it should feel sharp to the touch.

To use the scraper, set the tip into the scribed line at the far side of the sheet and pull the tool toward you, applying pressure with your thumb. It's easy for the tool to jump out of the groove, so don't press down too hard at first; if it skitters off sideways, you'll make a nasty scratch. As the groove gets deeper, you can increase the pressure.

Scraping is slow, but will always yield a successful groove if you work carefully.

5. Filing

Use as large a file as possible and start by holding it at a steep angle against the edge of the metal. For a right-angle bend on a narrow strip, I like to use a square file or the corner of a flat file. Cut a series of strokes, raising the handle end slightly with each stroke until the file lays flat across the workpiece. The effect is to create a V-shaped

SCRAPING A GROOVE

1 To make a scraper from an old file, heat the tang and bend it to roughly a 90° angle. The tip should be filed to shape before making the bend.

2 Drag the sharpened scraper along the groove, pressing down with enough force to tear up small shavings. Continue until a slight bulge appears on the underside.

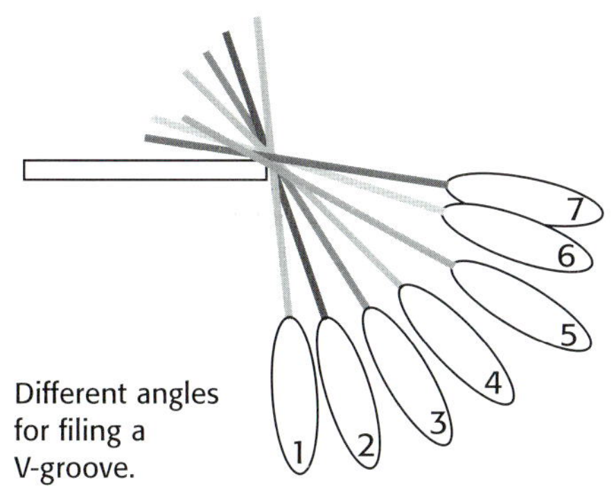

Different angles for filing a V-groove.

groove that grows from the edge toward the center. When it reaches about halfway across the sheet, turn the metal around and repeat the process from the other side. This simple method prevents the file from skating sideways across the sheet, something that is almost guaranteed to happen if you start by laying the file flat onto the sheet.

Jennifer Schellenbach, box. Copper, steel screen, timing ring, 7"H x 12"W x 6"D.

FILING A GROOVE

1 To file the groove, start by holding the file at a steep angle. This will allow it to "bite" the edge and prevent sliding sideways.

2 After filing a groove from one end, turn the strip around and start from the other side.

3 To modify a needle file to reach the inner part of a groove, heat it to red and press it against a soldering block to curve it slightly. Be sure a corner of the file is facing out, away from the curve.

4 This shows the curved needle file being used to complete a filed groove. This tool is also handy for opening out a groove cut with a separating disk.

Deborah Krupenia, *Tagasode II (Whose Sleeves?)*. Colored golds, sterling, Japanese copper alloys, 3/4"H x 3"W x 3 1/2"L, photos: Dean Powell.

Take time to cut the groove almost all the way through the metal; if you stop too soon, you'll get a rounded corner. Turn the piece over periodically to check your progress. When the groove is deep enough, a slightly raised line will appear on the reverse. Resist the temptation to test your work by bending the piece. It's fragile and will break if it's bent and opened too often.

When working on a wider strip—say, over an inch—it can be a little awkward to reach the midsection. Here's an easy trick: select a square or triangular needle file that you can dedicate to this purpose. Heat the file to bright red at a point about a half inch from the tip while grasping the handle section in pliers or vise grips. When the file is red, press it against a soldering block to bend the tip into a gentle curve, something like the shape of a ski. Be certain to bend so a corner (rather than a face) of the file is on the outer edge. Quench the file in water to harden it. This curve will reach nicely into a groove to widen and refine it.

Jon Michael Route, lidded box. Pewter, brass, copper, 1½"H x 9"W x 5"D.

Creating L-Shaped Pieces

Use one of the methods described above to score the line marked on the front-and-a-side strip. The goal is to make an L. When the groove is almost all the way through, you will be able to bend the panel with your fingers. The corner will crease with little pressure, creating a sharply defined edge visible on the back of the sheet. Never use a hammer or mallet to bend a scored corner. It's unnecessary, and to do so risks marring the metal and distorting its shape. If the piece doesn't bend in your fingers, the scoring isn't deep enough.

Bend the panel to a right angle

MAKING THE L-SHAPED PIECES

1 To test a groove, press the sides lightly; they should reveal a sharp edge when bent even a small distance. Do not try this too often or the scored groove will break.

2 Fill the groove by flowing in a piece of hard solder as soon as possible. Avoid doing other work on the panel until strengthening the corner, or the piece may break.

3 Cut one leg to the intended length, then set it nose-to-nose with its partner to transfer the dimension. File both edges until they are clean, square and even.

Kristina Kada, *Safety Zone*, container. Sterling, 1 1/2"H x 1"W x 1"D, photos: Ralph Gabriner. The box was cut from a single piece of sheet in the shape of a plus sign. After piercing the windows, the sides were bent and soldered. Details were applied and stamped.

and check it against a try square. (That's where the name comes from: to "try" or test the angle.) Adjust the angle to exactly 90°, then paint the inside of the joint with flux and set the piece aside on the soldering block. Repeat the process with the other panel. To reinforce the corners, lay one or two pieces of hard solder into each corner and heat evenly until the solder flows along the groove.

We now have two identical L-shaped pieces. If the score was precisely 90° from the edges, the two legs of the L are in the same plane. Lay the square along the bent edge (the corner of the box) to check this. If the legs are not correct, now is the time to scribe a line and saw away extra metal as needed to make the unit square in every dimension. Repeat this test (and correction, if needed) on the other L-shaped leg unit.

Measure the shorter leg of one of the pieces to the desired length, in this case 1" (about 2.5 cm). Mark the correct length and use a square to scribe a line that is perpendicular to the edge. Cut and file to make this edge straight and clean, then set this piece nose-to-nose with its partner, as shown on page 17. Transfer the measurement to the second unit and cut it to match.

Construction Sequence

A familiar question in box construction concerns the sequence of making the box and lid. One school of thought is to build a single unit to the size of the finished box, then cut the lid portion off after construction is complete. The advantage of this method is that any irregularity in the box segment is automatically created in the lid portion at the same time. If one goes out of square, the other does too, so they'll still match. A disadvantage is that cutting the two pieces apart is not easy. Because the blade is cutting in two places at once—at the top and bottom of the form or on two facing sides—the saw can easily wander off the line.

The other solution is to lay out and construct the lid and box in identical but separate operations. This has the advantage of allowing

CUTTING THE BOX AND LID

1 When both L's are soldered, measured and cleaned, lay out the division between lid and box and saw the pieces apart.

2 If the pieces have right angles and the opposing ends are the same length, the frame will be a symmetrical rectangle, guaranteed.

clean edges and easier forming, but requires careful work to ensure that the pieces fit.

I prefer a middle course: I lay out the box and lid together but cut them apart before forming. In other words, before I connect the two L's, I saw along the line that divides the lid from the bottom of the box, cutting each L into a tall and a short section, for the box and lid respectively. If this cut wavers badly, it will be difficult to keep the box symmetrical, so make every effort to cut precisely.

When we arrange the two L-shaped pieces to make a rectangle, the beauty of using this sequence becomes clear. Because the two shorter legs are exactly the same length, the two longer pieces (the front and back) have no choice but to be parallel. It's foolproof! The only decision left to be made is the length of the box, which in this example is 1⁵/₈" (about 4 cm). Make a tiny scratch on the top edge, just past that point, and position the pieces on a flat soldering block. Flux both corners and apply a few chips of hard solder on the outside of the two joints. The excess metal will be cut away after soldering.

Use a generous flame and move it back and forth over the box to develop an even heat. The goal is to bring both units to soldering temperature simultaneously. Remove the flame as soon as the solder flows, then quench the piece in water. Allow the work to soak in pickle for a few minutes, then rinse the piece in water and inspect the joints to be certain the solder has flowed completely.

Chuck Evans, *Hollow Form #1*. Sterling, 3" cube.

Inserting the Panels

Now that we have a frame it would be possible to simply set it onto a sheet of metal, solder it down and trim off the excess to complete the box. Except in the case of very small boxes, I prefer to fit the panel inside the walls. This process takes a little longer, but it's worth the effort for three reasons:

1. When a wall frame simply sits on top of a panel during soldering, warping is almost inevitable. Even when subtle, warped walls can push the box out of square (or round, or oval, etc.). This will cause the box and lid to make a poor fit.
2. It's also very common for the bottom to warp when heated in this way, preventing the box from sitting flat. This problem is so common that almost every container that sits on a table, from paper cups to fine china, has a rim or "foot" to reduce the contact surface. With an inset bottom, only the frame touches; this rim is quite easy to make flat.
3. With geometrically regular boxes (squares, rectangles, ovals and so on), it's relatively easy to achieve a perfectly shaped bottom panel with careful cutting and filing. Regular shapes like these can be made with layout tools such as a T-square, ruler and dividers, or with commer-

Talya Baharal, *The Hieroglyph Within*, locket. Sterling, 2¾"H x 2"W x 1⅝"D, photo: Will Faller.

cially made plastic templates. Craftspeople familiar with computer drawing programs might also find it efficient to draw the panels on screen and then glue the printout onto the metal sheet.

An advantage of this technique is that work on the panel is independent of the frame. If the shape gets wrecked in the sawing process, it's easy enough to start over with a new piece, without having damaged the wall frame. It's also a simple matter to lay the top and bottom panels together to be certain they match. By squeezing the "perfect" rectangle into the frame, you know with certainty that the box will be correct.

All these benefits depend on a tight fit between the wall frame and panel. It should take firm pressure with both hands to force the panel into place—fingers, but no tools. If you need a hammer to tap the panel into position, the fit is too tight. Forcing the panel will make it buckle. Instead, pull it out, file the edges a stroke or two, and try again. Proceed slowly so you don't make the frustrating mistake of taking too much metal away. As you approach a good fit, file a bevel on the edges sloping toward the outside of the box. This will provide a space for the solder to run.

To ensure that the recess is uniform, set a small flat object like a coin or piece of popsicle stick under the box and press down until the panel is touching the support. I usually place the solder on the shallow side of the recess, i.e., the underside of the box (or the top of the lid), but unless the box is so deep that it will hamper the flame control, either side will work.

Apply flux to both sides of the panel and set chips of solder around the edge. It's better to use several small pieces of solder rather than fewer large pieces, since smaller pieces melt sooner. Use as little solder as possible; because of the tight fit, very little will

INSERTING THE BOTTOM PANEL

1 Saw out the bottom, a rectangle that makes a tight fit in the frame. File as necessary to make the bottom snap into place.

2 Use a coin or scrap of sheet metal to ensure that the depth of the bottom is uniform. The box could be inverted with the coin out of sight beneath, then the wooden dowel would be used to press the bottom panel down onto the coin.

Tim McCreight, container. Stainless steel, wood, pebble, 3"H, photo: Jay York.

Mariko Kusumoto, *Homeland*. Sterling, copper, brass, found objects, 7$\frac{5}{8}$"H x 5$\frac{1}{4}$"W x 1$\frac{3}{4}$"D, photo: M. Lee Fatherree. "When I think about my temple, I remember the antique paintings with their faded colors, the hollows in the stone steps that four hundred years of rain dripping from the roof has created, and the dark colors of wood grain and old metal."

be needed and extra solder will mar the surface. As before, heat the entire box and floor panel evenly and remove the torch as soon as the solder flows. Repeat the process for the lid. You'll end up with two units that are identical except for their differing heights.

Completing the Box

At this point you could turn to the second chapter of this book to select an appropriate hinge, then choose one of the catches from the third chapter to complete the project. But as anyone who has opened a shoe box knows, hinges and catches are not essential to every box.

To complete this box in a simple but elegant manner, start by refining the interface edges, the place

Jane Martin, box. Sterling, copper, brass, nickel, 2" cube, photo: Doug Yaple.

where the top edge of the box touches the bottom edge of the lid. Lay a piece of sandpaper on a tabletop or other flat surface and slide the box across it. This process is made both easier and more effective by taping or gluing sheets of sandpaper onto pieces of Masonite or Plexiglas. Three rectangles with sandpaper glued onto each side will provide a sequence of six grits. Move systematically from the coarsest to the finest (typically 80, 120, 220, 320, 400, 600) to create edges that are uniform, flat and free of marks. Rub the edges of both the box and the lid until all edges are smooth.

To secure the lid onto the box, you can make an interior lip, or *bezel*. In the example, a bezel is attached to the lid, but it can just as easily be attached to the box. Use a thin gauge of sheet metal (the example uses 26-gauge sterling) about 2 mm wider than the interior height of the lid. This is marked, scored and bent to make a thin frame that will fit snugly into the lid, and then soldered into place. The solder should catch the bezel at several points around the lid but need not flow in a continuous join.

Ken Weston, cigarette box with holder. Sterling, 14K green gold.

COMPLETING THE RECTANGULAR BOX

1 Rub the box onto sandpaper of increasing fineness to make the edges true and smooth.

2 An interior bezel is cut and fit all the way into the lid and extends just enough to grip the inside lip of the box.

3 The finished bezel can be adjusted by rubbing it with any blunt tool to press it in or out as needed to make the correct fit.

Marcia A. Macdonald, *You Don't Keep Secrets… They Keep You, Box #1.* Wood, copper, brass, 4"H x 3$\frac{1}{2}$"W x 4$\frac{1}{4}$"D, photo: Richard Gehrke.

Merideth Malony, locket. Sterling, copper, brass, 1 1/2"H. "This is a voyeuristic view of a bathroom, intentionally awkward and uncomfortable. The texture implies wooden walls; the chain is a reference to old-fashioned toilet pull chains."

Micki Lippe, *Spirit House,* pendant container. Sterling, 22K, 1 1/2"H, photo: Richard Nicol. "The poles that support the roof of this symbolic house were inspired by those used in Japanese houses. The piece is assembled by soldering; the chain slides through a tube hidden under the roof."

Using a thin sheet allows for easy adjustment to tighten the lid. After soldering and cleanup, press the lid onto the box. If it's too loose or too tight, use a burnisher to press the bezel inward or outward as needed to correct the problem. As the bezel wears over years of use, adjusting the tension will be just this easy.

Making Cylinders

Making a straight-walled cylinder is more challenging than it might at first appear. First, it's the nature of a metal sheet, when bent into a cylinder, to deform more at the edges than in the center. This phenomenon is sometimes evident in a finger ring and becomes increasingly obvious as the size of the cylinder grows. An extreme example is illustrated below.

Kristina Kada, pill box. Sterling, 1/2"H x 1"Dia, photo: Ralph Gabriner. The lid is secured by the friction of an interior bezel. The openings were cut with a chisel; details at the seam were added with stamping tools.

A second problem stems from the fact that many of the tools we use to make forms round are tapered. To make a ring round, for instance, we slide it along a tapered mandrel until it snugs up against the taper. In the case of a tall cylinder, this means that only the top and bottom edges can be made round. For this reason, a collection of untapered mandrels—like steel rods and pipes—is useful when making cylinders.

Lapped Joints

A cylinder is made by bending a strip of sheet metal until the ends meet. Bringing the two edges together makes a *butt joint*—but this solution is difficult to accomplish and structurally weak. It's better to overlap the edges, a process that dramatically increases the surface area brought into the seam.

Though the difference appears small, a *lapped joint* has at least five times the surface contact of a butt joint. Obviously, if the sheet is simply overlapped, the joint area will be twice as thick as the rest of the cylinder. To compensate for this,

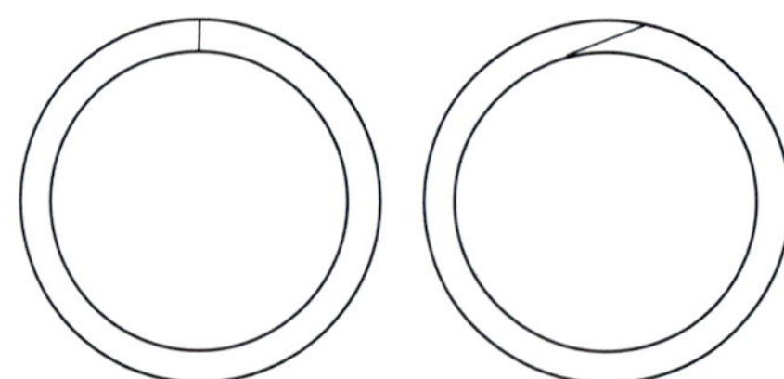

planish an area about 1/4" wide on each edge of the panel, tapering it paper-thin at the edge. This is called *scarfing*. Smooth out the hammer marks by filing, and trim the outer edges where hammering has spread the form.

Closing a cylinder with a lapped joint brings a special problem: when you cinch the form with wire to pull it tight, the edges tend to slide past one another. To get around this, use a ruler or dividers to mark short lines equidistant from the top and bottom edges. Saw along these lines to just more than half the width of the scarfed section. Either use a large saw blade or cut away a very slim V at each of the four locations.

Bend the cylinder into a forming block or sandbag. There are many ways to do this, all variations on the method shown here. I've used a steel-ring mandrel and a leather sandbag, striking the rod with a mallet to force it into a cylinder. Pliers are used to bend the "fingers" on one side upward to engage with the fingers of the other side. Slide the cylinder onto a dowel, pipe, or similar form, and strike the joint with a mallet to press the fingers firmly onto each other. Wrap the form with binding wire, twisting it tight enough to se-

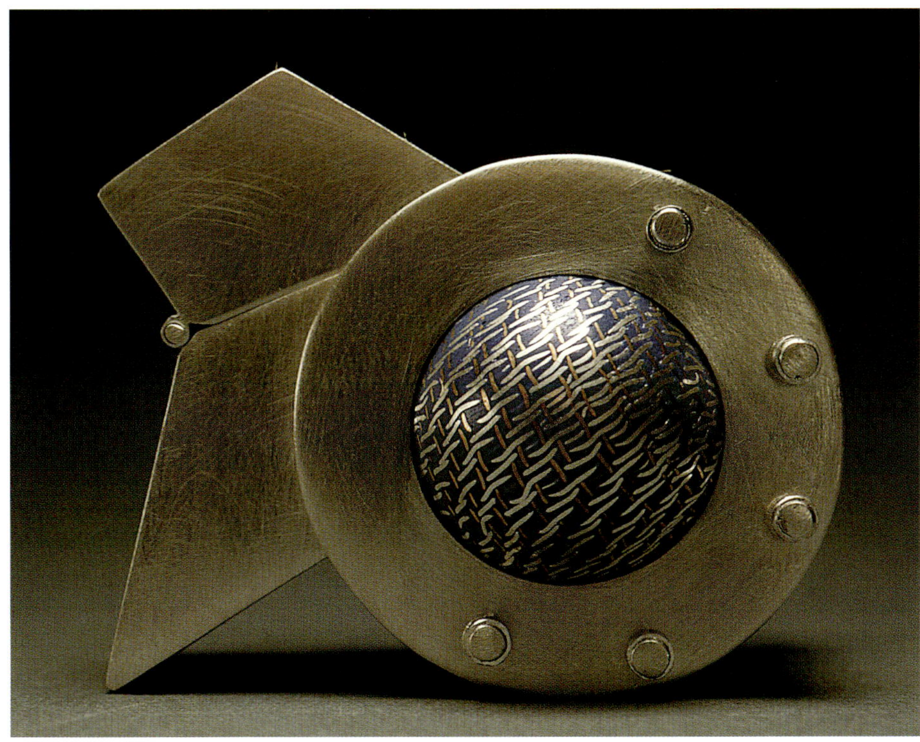

Steve A. Musselman, snuff box. Sterling, copper, woven fine silver, enamel, $1^{1}/_{4}$"H x $1^{3}/_{4}$"W.

cure the cylinder for soldering. As the joint is pulled tight and the fingers engage, the edges are prevented from sliding past each other.

Flux the seam inside and out, apply solder and heat evenly. After pickling, rinsing and drying, slide the cylinder onto a steel mandrel and planish with a steel hammer to even it out further.

Crimped Joints

On any given day, we all see remarkable examples of seamed cylinders. We call them tin cans and take them for granted, but they are the result of years of research and engineering evolution. Though there are many styles, let's look at the most familiar method used to form a can; from there, you can devise your own variations.

MAKING A LAPPED JOINT CYLINDER

1 As a first step in making a lap joint, the panel is hammered at both ends to thin it, a process called scarfing.

2 Bend the sheet up by striking a steel rod into a bag filled with sand, often used as a soft and pliable support for bending metal.

3 Continue until the cylinder pulls up into shape.

(continued on next page)

Start by bending one end of a sheet metal panel onto itself and inserting a strip of metal to prevent this fold from closing completely. To do this, scribe a line parallel to the edge (in the example, it's inset 1/4") and go over the line repeatedly with a scribe to make a groove. With the metal overhanging a sharp edge, strike it with a mallet to start the bend. Fold the sheet metal and insert a metal spacer equal to the width of the fold (1/4") and long enough so that it sticks out slightly from each end. Grasp the folded area in a vise and bend it 90° to create the configuration shown in the example. Then bend a single 1/4" fin on the opposite end.

Bend the metal around to make a cylinder and insert the short flap into the bent-over, longer flap. Crimp the joint closed against an anvil or in a vise. Set the cylinder on a steel mandrel and pound the crimped joint flat onto the form. In some cases it may be necessary to add a bit of solder. When properly made, this is a very tight joint.

Dies

Cutting Dies

Most cutting tools (scissors, knives, etc.) are freehand devices. They are as accurate as the person using them. This is not the case with a cutting die, a tool that carries a specific silhouette and will reproduce it exactly over and over again. If you've ever cut out gingerbread men, you understand how a cutting die works.

In metalworking, the process is slightly more complicated because the tools need to be made of hardened steel and held in perfect alignment. The photograph on this

MAKING A LAPPED JOINT CYLINDER *(continued)*

4 Lift and lower opposing tabs so they can engage. This will prevent the cylinder from simply rolling itself smaller as the joint is cinched with wire.

5 Use a stout binding wire to pull the edges tightly together. Brush flux into the joint, then use a mallet to pound the seam flat for soldering.

6 Disks have been soldered into place for the bottom and top. The surface should be cleaned up with a file.

7 This is the finished box. A stand-off hinge was made by soldering a piece of sheet onto the rim of both the lid and the box.

A circle cutter is a kind of cutting die. A hammer blow is used to force a punch through a sheet with the help of matching plates—one above and one below the metal being cut.

MAKING A CRIMPED JOINT

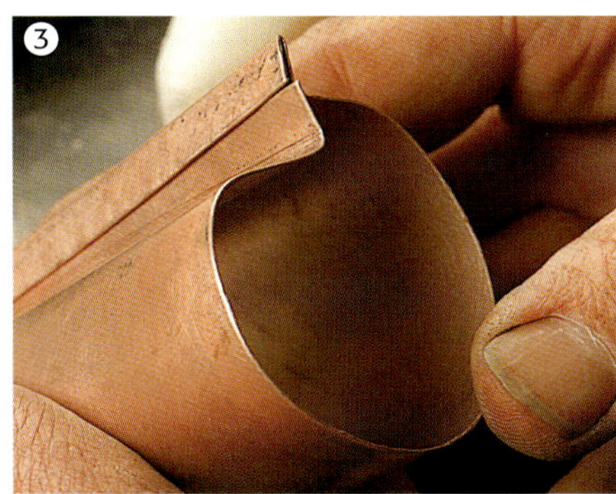

1 Bend the edge of the panel over a sharp corner with a mallet.

2 Continue bending the strip, this time with a piece of metal (here, brass) temporarily in place to prevent the fold from closing up entirely.

3 After making a single bend on the other end, roll the panel into a cylinder and slide the two folds together.

4 Mallet the crimped joint onto a stake to make it flat. It can be soldered or left as a cold connection.

page shows a *disk cutter*, perhaps the most common cutting die used by metalsmiths. The tool consists of two identical plates of thick steel that are pierced with round holes in several sizes. These two plates are held parallel and slightly apart by a steel spacer. For each hole there is a hardened steel rod (called a *punch*) of exactly the same diameter. In order to make a clean cut, the punch must be a tight fit through the hole.

To use a disk cutter, start by setting it onto a solid surface—preferably not a steel anvil, because this would damage both the die and the anvil. A length of tree trunk or wooden beam makes an excellent working surface. Slide the metal to be cut into the die, sighting through the hole to locate it properly, then slide the correct punch into place so it rests on the metal. Avoid tapping the punch as if you are driving a nail; at each tap, the sheet metal will move slightly, almost guaranteeing a ragged edge and scarred surface. Strike the top of the die with a large hammer, the goal being to force the punch through the sheet in a single blow.

It's not unusual for the punch to become stuck in the die. Don't try to pound it through! The top of the punch mushrooms out in use, so any efforts to force it through will only press it more tightly into the hole, damaging both parts of the tool. Instead, turn the die over and pound the punch out with a wooden dowel. It's tempting to use a smaller punch for this job (because it's right there), but don't do it.

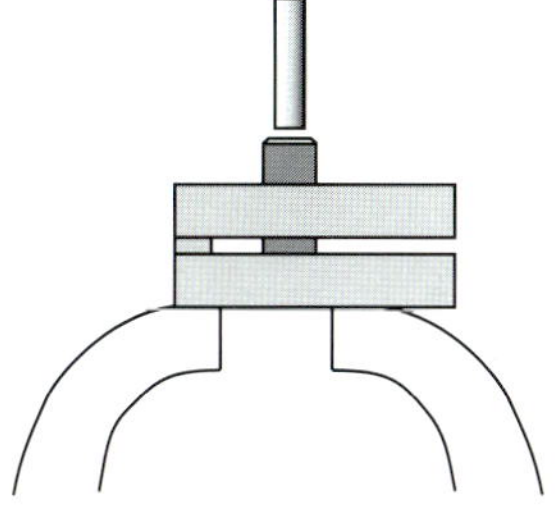

You'll severely damage both the punch that's stuck *and* the one you were using to drive it back. I like to set the die over the slightly opened jaws of a large vise. This allows the punch to drop safely out as soon as it's loosened.

Conforming Dies

Forming dies are used to form metal. *Con*forming dies consist of two parts that fit together, i.e., conform to each other. These are used industrially to stamp out thousands of items, from spoons to car fenders. Generally, the high cost of having a conforming die made from steel is prohibitive unless many pieces are being made. Fortunately for us, the most generic conforming die, a *dapping die*, is sold at a relatively low cost. It's used to transform a disk of sheet metal into a dome.

Dapping dies are sometimes made in brass and wood, but the best version is a steel cube, usually 2" or $2^{1}/_{2}$" on each side, into which hemispherical depressions of various sizes have been cut. The die block is really only half the die; it needs a matching element called a *dapping punch* to complete the tool. Punches come in sets that match the various depressions and are typically purchased together with the dies.

A dapping die and punches belong to the family of conforming dies, tools that press a relatively malleable material between a positive and negative of the same form, in this case a dome.

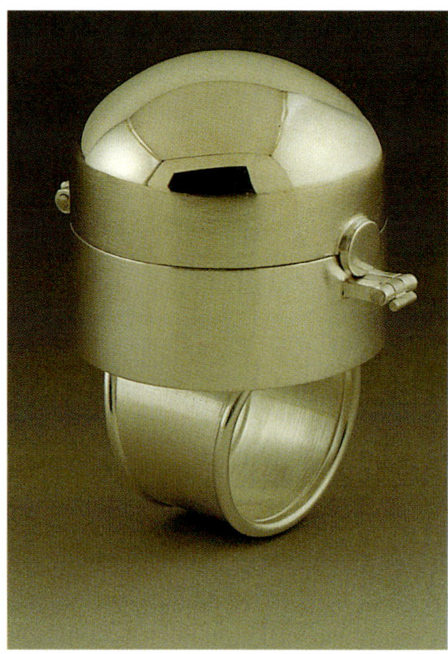

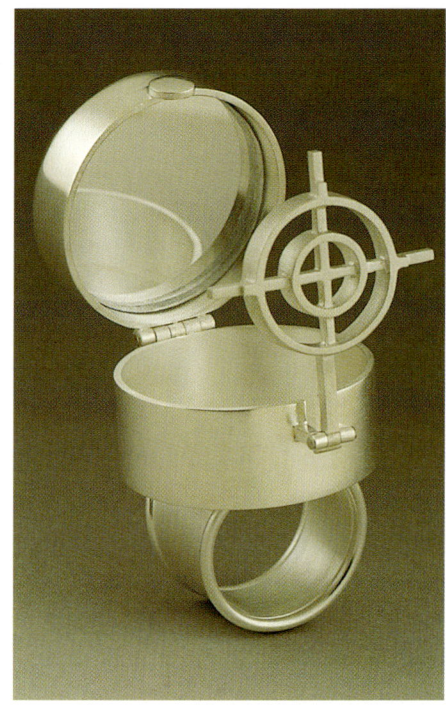

Tara Stephenson, *Sight #3*, ring/compact. Sterling, mirror, $2^{1}/_{4}$"H x 1"W x 1"D.

To use this die, select a cavity larger than the disk being formed and choose a punch that *almost* makes a snug fit; there should be enough room between the block and the punch to allow for the thickness of the metal. Set the die on a solid table, position the metal disk in the hole, and strike the punch down on it with a medium-weight hammer. Strike a couple of blows, listening for the solid thump that tells you the punch has hit the die or "bottomed out." To increase the curve, move the cup to a smaller die and use the appropriate punch to repeat the process. Continue moving down the sequence of die holes until the desired curve is achieved, annealing between steps if necessary.

Nonconforming Dies

If a conforming die is defined as a tool that *imposes* its form on metal, a nonconforming die might be described as a tool that *lends* its form. These dies, also called *silhouette dies,* consist of a cut-out area in a rigid form. Unlike the dapping block, this open area has no floor. The metal is temporarily held against the die and a variety of tools are used to press the metal downward.

With nonconforming dies, the outer dimension—the silhouette—will always be the same, but the volume can be different with each pressing, depending on how the tools are used. It's possible to get consistent results with nonconforming dies, but part of their value lies in the fact that different effects are possible. The edge will always be the same, which means a

Albion Smith, pocket watch. Sterling, fine silver, amethyst, sapphire, photos: Carol Holaday.

box and lid will automatically match, but the third dimension that grows out of the silhouette can vary widely.

The following examples show the use of conforming and nonconforming dies.

Using a Conforming Die to Make a Locket

Create two identical domes by using a dapping die as described above. Each dome will be soldered into a "wall" (a metal ring) to make the front and back of a locket. To ensure a neat appearance after soldering, rub the bottom edge of each dome on sandpaper to make it flat. File around the circumference of both domes to create a vertical edge that will make a solid connection to the wall.

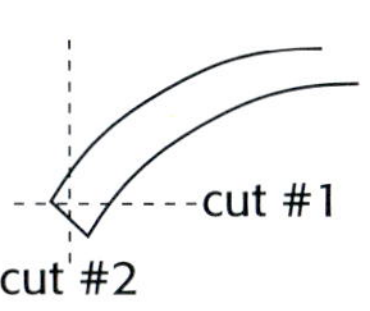

Cut two identical strips from sheet metal; I've used 20-gauge (.8 mm) in the example. The correct length can be calculated mathematically by multiplying the diameter times "π" (pi, 3.14). Add the equivalent of two thicknesses of the metal, and you'll be very close to the mark. Alternately, wrap the strip around the dome as if measuring a bezel for a stone. Cut these two strips with shears or a saw, taking care that the edges are parallel. Form the strips into rings and solder them closed with hard solder. True up the rings on a mandrel to make them perfectly round, and test the fit against the domes. At this point, the domes shouldn't *quite* fit inside the rings. If the rings are too small, they can be stretched by forcing them along the mandrel with a mallet. If they are too large, cut out a piece of metal and resolder the joint.

You may want to make a delicate interior rim inside the locket. Here's how. Set the domes aside and use a small-gauge square wire to make rings that will just fit inside the wall frame. If you don't have a square drawplate or square wire on hand, make the ring from round wire and leave it a tiny bit too large. Solder the loop and planish it lightly on an anvil. File the circumference to create a flat outer edge; at the same time, reduce the size of the loop so that it fits neatly into the wall. Press the ring all the way in and solder each rim wire with hard solder.

This drawing shows the cross section with the interior rim (shaded areas) in place.

Now press the domes into place, making sure they have an identical recess. If a dome is loose, planish the edge of the dome against a dapping punch held in a vise to stretch it. As the pieces approach the correct size—and there is typically some stretching and filing neces-

MAKING A LOCKET WITH A CONFORMING DIE

1 Make the outer rims of this locket by bending around two identical strips of sheet metal.

2 A rim for the inside of the locket is made by planishing a ring of round wire. Note the high polish on the planishing hammer. This is the finish that will be transferred to the ring.

3 If the interior rim is too large, it can be marked with a saw while in place inside the wall of the locket. The rim wire is cut, resoldered and fitted into the wall.

4 The rim is then soldered into position with hard solder.

5 The dome is carefully trimmed to make a pressure fit into the ring. Patience and care in this stage will make a much nicer locket.

6 Use very small bits of solder to connect the dome to the walls; since the fitting was precise, only a small amount is needed. Too much solder will make a messy joint that will be difficult to clean.

sary to achieve this—clean the inside of the ring with Scotch-Brite. That way, when the pieces snap together, you'll be ready to solder.

Press the pieces together, flux inside and out, and place six or seven small bits of hard solder around the circumference. Heat as broadly as possible so the solder will flow uniformly around the entire joint.

In the case of a locket, your two pieces will usually be identical. To make a box, follow the same plan but make one wall taller than the other and use a flat disk as the floor in that unit. To complete the locket, select a hinge and a clasp from later chapters of this book. The cradle hinge is the traditional choice for a round locket or box, but you may find that other styles of hinges suit your design better.

Abrasha, locket. Stainless steel, 18K, diamonds, 1 3/8"Dia. A tube rivet at the top of the piece allows the sections to rotate open and simultaneously provides a place for the bail. The stainless steel parts (which are machined on a lathe) make a dramatic contrast with the gold and diamonds.

Making a Box with a Nonconforming Die

The beauty of a conforming die (like the dapping block used in the preceding example) is that it gives identical units every time. The disadvantage is the same: the die will create identical units, every time. This is great for efficiency, but it can put a strain on creativity.

As described above, a nonconforming die creates a consistent, repeatable outer edge while allowing wide variation in the contour of the form. Let's look at the steps for making an asymmetrical box using a nonconforming die.

Draw a silhouette of the top view of the box: in this case a modified rectangle with rounded corners. In this example, the same die is used to create both the top and bottom of a pillbox, but it would be possible to construct the box by scoring and folding sheet metal, then using a die to make a matching lid. If that were the case, I'd make the box first and then trace it onto the die block.

MAKING A BOX WITH A NONCONFORMING DIE

1 Dies can be made of nothing more complicated than Masonite glued to plywood or particle board. Sawing is done with a spiral saw blade. Note the paper template.

2 Attach the annealed sheet to the die with short flat-head screws.

3 Start by tapping a large dapping punch over the sheet to locate the opening of the die. Work concentrically to press the metal down into the die hole.

(continued on next page)

Short-use dies can be made from sheets of plastic or wood, or by layering both together to create a material that is economical, easy to saw, and capable of holding a crisp edge. In this case, I've used a piece of 1/4" tempered Masonite glued onto 1/2" plywood. If the form will be used many times—and particularly if the edge of the form must be sharp—substitute plastic (e.g., Plexiglas) for the Masonite.

Draw the form on the block and drill a hole inside the line. Use a

jeweler's sawframe or coping saw to cut along the line, then refine the edges by filing. When making a symmetrical form like this one, it's possible to use only one side of the die, so the underside can be left irregular. With asymmetrical forms, both sides of the die will be used, and the walls must be exactly vertical. If they tilt, the opening on one side will be larger than the opening on the other. To check this, trace the hole onto a piece of paper with a pencil, then flip the die over and trace it again. The two outlines should be a perfect match.

This process requires a piece of metal that is at least 1/2" larger all

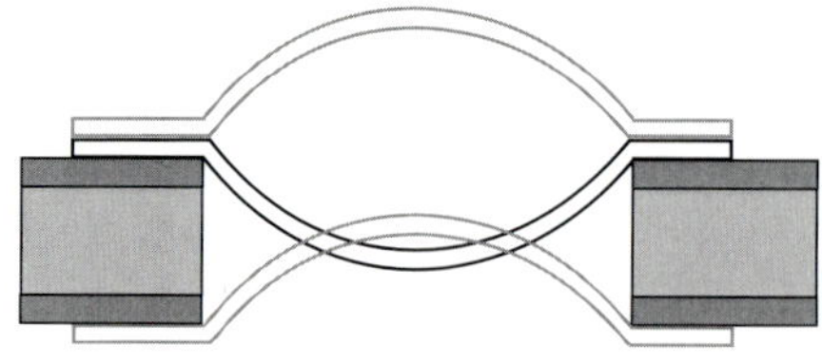

around than the opening. The part of the sheet that sits on top of the die is called the *flange;* it's a skirt that is a necessary byproduct of die forming. The flange can be cut away entirely after the forming is finished, but it can also be used to good advantage. In this example, I've used it to add interest to the design and to provide a straight edge for the hinge.

The box in the example is made with 20-gauge sheet. It's worth noting that die forming usually allows a slightly thinner metal to be used than would be recommended for other forming methods, since the stress of deformation is distributed throughout the sheet.

Use screws to secure the metal temporarily to the die. Locate the screws around the form and drill small pilot holes. A shallow form like the one being made here will need only one screw for each side, but deep forms will need to be attached at each corner as well. Lay a piece of paper on the die and rub it with the side of a pencil point to locate the die opening and holes. Use this as a guide to cut out a piece of metal and mark the location of each screw hole. Use a drill and saw to make a hole equal to or a little larger than the shaft of the screw. (Note: it's dangerous to drill a large hole in sheet metal. The bit is very likely to snag on the metal and pull it from your hands. Instead, drill a small hole, no more than 1/16", then use a saw to create a hole large enough for the screw. This process is *much* safer; please take the extra time to use it.)

Screw the metal firmly onto the die and tap it with a mallet or the handle of a ball peen hammer to locate the edges of the die hole. Use a

MAKING A BOX WITH A NONCONFORMING DIE *(continued)*

4 The form can be modeled to many contours by changing tools and altering the direction and force of the blows. Remove the metal and anneal it as necessary.

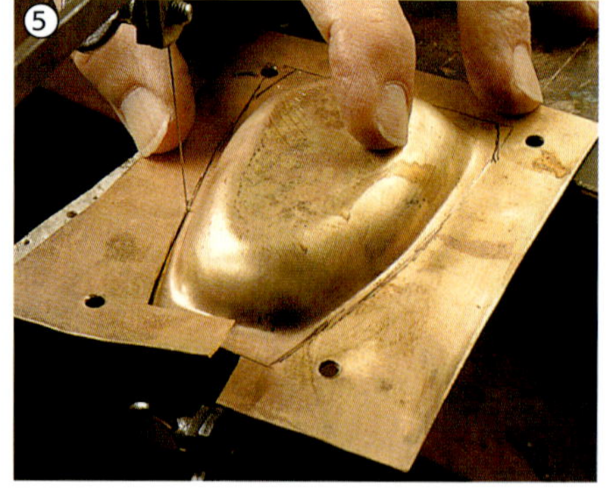

5 When the form is complete the flange is sawn off, except for sections that might be used for hinges, catches or decoration.

6 The finished box. The catch swings open on a pivot to release the lid.

Adam "Monkey Shines" Clark, *Lovers Luck Lost, Liberty Lie*, container. Fine silver, garnets, quartz, glass eye, carved bone, 6"H x 4"Dia.

large dapping punch (or a similarly shaped piece of wooden dowel) to outline the form. In this box I want a shape that is contoured at the edges but flat for most of the floor. When a deep form like this is desired, direct the blows in concentric circles, always using punches that are as large as possible. If annealing is necessary, remove the screws, anneal the sheet, and reattach the form to the die. An electric screwdriver, while hardly a necessity, is a welcome tool for this step.

The beauty of a nonconforming die is that it allows for different depths in the lid and base. In the example, the lower piece is deeper

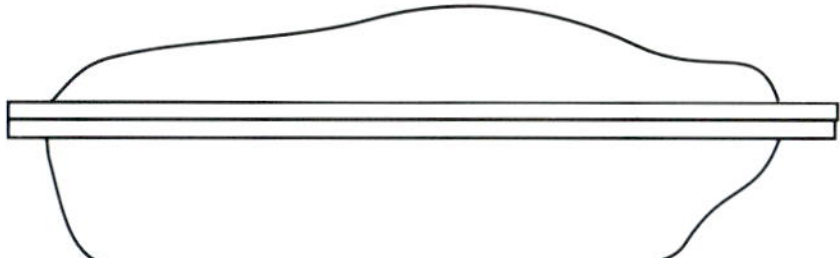

and more regular than the top. After forming the first unit to the depth I wanted, I've laid a straightedge across the form and measured the depth with a ruler. Then I jotted this down for comparison with the other half. Of course it's also

Jan Baum, *Guide #4 Celastrus Scandens*, locket pendant. Sterling, celastrus scandens fruit, cultured pearls, nickel silver, glass, $1\frac{1}{4}$"Dia, photos: Phil Harris.

possible to approach this more spontaneously, working the metal into the die until it intuitively seems right.

When both pieces have been formed, remove them from the die and set them upside down onto a flat surface. If they are warped, it's easy to press the flange flat with a mallet. Select a location for the hinge on one of the pieces and scribe a straight line with a ruler. Then use a saw to remove the rest of the flange. Set the pieces together, trace the outline of the first piece onto the second, and cut away the unneeded flange on the second piece.

Any of the hinges described in Chapter 2 can be used on this box.

Using a Hydraulic Press

An alternate way to use silhouette dies is with the aid of a car jack and a sturdy steel frame. The concept is the same as with dies used manually, but the force is applied when the pressure of the jack brings two steel plates together.

The hydraulic press manufactured by Bonny Doon Engineering.

Advantages of a Press

- More pressure can be created.
- Less physical effort is required.
- More consistent results are possible.
- Less stress on the metal allows the use of thinner gauges.
- The sheet does not need to be attached to the die.
- Because the force is broadly distributed, the process is less likely to damage patterned metal.

The Press

A hydraulic press is relatively simple. Two vertical posts are welded to a base plate with a bar perma-

Carol Webb, *Willie's Box*. Photo-etched copper over fine silver, $4\frac{1}{4}$"H x $2\frac{1}{4}$"Dia.

nently attached across at the top. A horizontal plate is mounted inside the frame in such a way that it can travel upwards. A hydraulic car jack is set inside the frame beneath the plate. When the ram of the jack (the part that pushes up, lifting the car) extends, it lifts the plate and presses whatever is on it against the top bar.

Though the parts are simple, a press frame must be very strong and perfectly square. The force being used is tremendous, so the possibility of injury is severe if the frame were to break. Only use frames purchased from a reputable dealer.

The dies used in a press can be identical to those used with hand methods, but many other variations are also possible. For more information I recommend the book *Hydraulic Die Forming for Jewelers & Metalsmiths* by Susan Kingsley.

These three forms were all created in the same die, all from the same thickness of metal. The only difference was the choice of urethane.

Using Urethane with a Hydraulic Press

In the box described above, the metal was pressed into the die with a rigid metal punch. It's possible to duplicate that process with the hydraulic press, but more often the punch is replaced with a pad of a tough rubber called *urethane*. As shown here, the urethane conforms to the die and presses the metal through the silhouette opening. In this example the die has determined the outer shape of the form, while the rubber pad—called the *ram* when used this way—assumes the shape of the die.

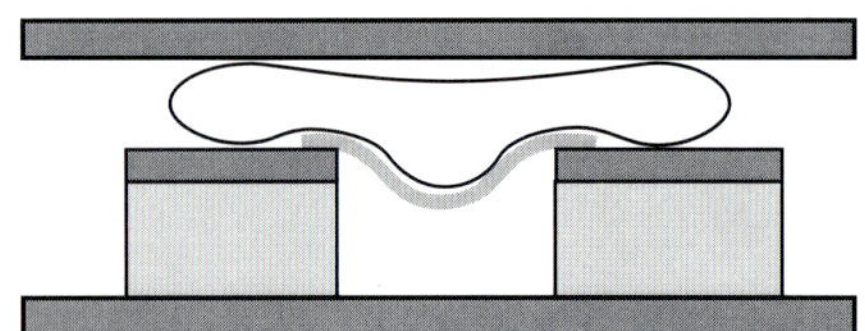

An alternate method reverses the parts: the punch becomes the

David Jones, *Keyed Seam Hut*, box. Sterling, 18K, fine silver, antique mother-of-pearl buttons, copper, 3½"H x 2¼"Dia, photo: Walker Montgomery.

Richard Finney, *Prairie Roots*. Copper, ivory, $2^{1}/_{4}$"H x 6"Dia.

rigid component, while the flexible urethane pad—in this case called a *matrix*—becomes the die. The punch can be made of any resilient material such as plastic, wood or

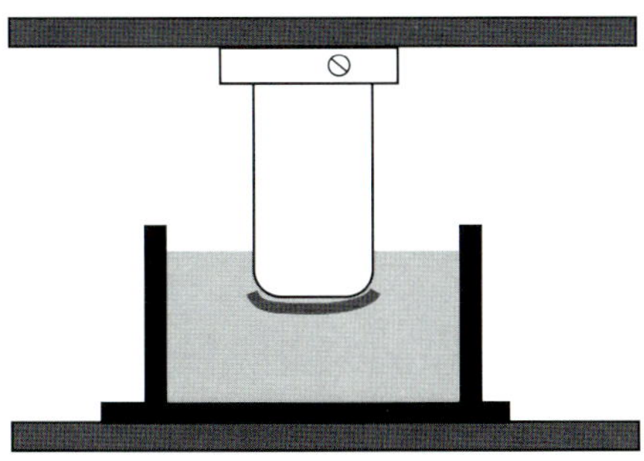

metal. Most metalworkers use acrylic or Delrin for their punches; these materials are inexpensive and easy to carve.

To develop the best detail, the urethane should be "contained" by trapping it in a stout container of some sort. For example, a section of 4" steel pipe might be welded to a steel base and fitted with a cylindrical pad of urethane. Trapping the pad in this way directs the force of the press back toward the ram, a process that ensures maximum detail.

Urethane pad is made in several grades of flexibility, identified in a measurement called *durometers*. The two most common versions are 80 durometer (yellow) and 95 durometer (red). Both are available in several thicknesses, generally from $^{1}/_{4}$" to 1". As you might guess, the deeper the form you want to create, the thicker the pad you should use. The harder pad (95) will yield a form with a flatter center and a steeper angle at the perimeter than the same die made with a softer urethane. The photo on page 38 shows three forms created in the same die with three grades (durometers) of urethane.

Left: Lorraine Lenskold, *God Box (To Put Your Troubles Into)*. Reticulated sterling, 14K, carved and dyed bone, $2^{1}/_{4}$"H x 1"W x $^{3}/_{8}$"D, photo: Ralph Gabriner.

Below: Frances J. Pickens, canister. Copper, $3^{3}/_{8}$"H x 4"Dia, photo: Paul Kodama.

Finishing Touches

Thickening the Rim

There is a split second of drama with almost every box or locket: the moment when the lid is lifted for the first time to reveal the interior. OK, no trumpets or drum roll ... but for all its subtlety, the view that presents itself at that moment has a serious impact on our response to the box.

One immediate reaction concerns the edge, since this is usually our first chance to observe the thickness of the material. Generally boxes are monolithic forms, objects characterized by their mass. When we lift the lid and peer inside, the illusion is dispelled. This can be good—boxes *should* have an inside!—but the perceived transi-

Advanced Uses of Dies

It's easy to see how dies can be used to make identical locket parts, but this is hardly the end of the story. Ingenious designers can find ways to use die-formed panels as segments of boxes. Die-formed units can also be sawn apart and recombined to make unusual forms. Though die forming is an ancient art, the modern steel-and-urethane method described here is encouraging a new generation of creative exploration.

A flat strip of brass was soldered into the completed box to create a thicker rim. In addition to making the box stronger, the visual weight of the rim gives the container increased drama.

tion from massive object to thin sheet can also be disappointing. By thickening the edge of a box or locket, we can suggest a more substantial object. At the same time, we make these treasured items stronger and extend their lives.

There are several ways to thicken the edge of a box or locket. The oval box above shows how rectangular bar can be used to thicken a rim. This can be done with com-

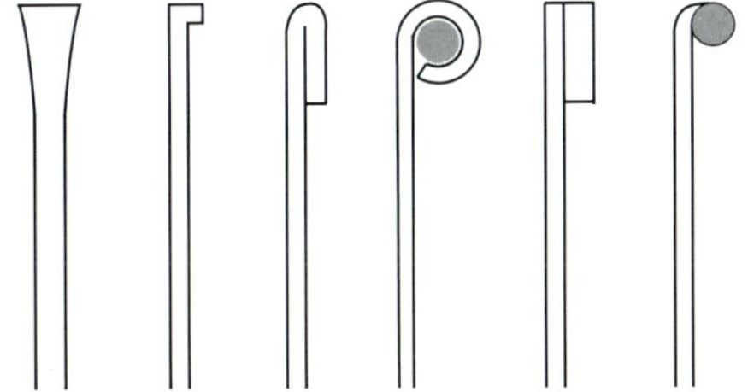

mercially made barstock (in gold, it might be called *sizing wire*) or with a strip you make yourself. Straighten a thick wire and planish it on an anvil as described below to make a rectangular bar.

When planishing, use a hammer with a highly polished, slightly domed face. Stand close to an anvil or similar steel plate, reach around to its far side and point the wire di-

Tina Chisena, container. African wonderstone, copper, brass, 3"H x 2¾"W x 1⅝"D, photo: Bill Branson. This box is made of soapstone and fitted with repousséd sections of brass/copper mokumé. The metal elements were soldered onto a base of thick copper. That unit was pinned and glued to the stone container.

rectly back at yourself. This position ensures that the hammer blows land flat, and it also reveals most clearly what happens when they don't. If the hammer is angled as it makes contact, the wire will curve away from the point of impact. This situation should be corrected immediately; otherwise, it will quickly get out of control.

Round wire can also be transformed into rectangular bar with a

Alan Perry, *Pebble Reliquary.* Bronze, 14K, jasper, lapis, 1"H x 2"W x 1¼"D, photo: Andrew Edgar.

rolling mill. When using a mill, start by planishing the tip to the desired size. This allows you to determine the optimum proportions and set the gap in the mill. Before rolling, take a moment to make certain the wire is perfectly straight. (Kinks and curves will be exaggerated by the rolling process.) If possible, keep tension on the wire both going into and coming out of the mill.

As illustrated earlier in the round locket example, an edge can be thickened by soldering in a metal ring. Make a hoop from round wire, true it up on a mandrel and flatten it with a hammer. Then file

Suzanne Pugh, *Boiler #2*, box. Sterling, fine silver, pearl, 8"H x 3"W x 3"D.

Elise Landry, *Reliquary*. Sterling, 2½"H x 4"W x 2½"D. Cast panels were assembled to make the box, which closes with a pressure-fit closing. The lid is domed and contains a cast thorn from a hawthorn tree trapped inside.

the edges to allow the ring to fit snugly inside the walls of the locket. The cross section of the thickening rim is rectangular, but I don't recommend starting with rectangular bar. While it's possible to bend a rectangle into a hoop, the process is difficult and requires repeated annealing. Starting with a round wire is both faster and easier.

Domed Disks

In some cases, particularly with smaller boxes, sheet metal is used to create an interior rim. In the example shown here, a domed disk is set onto a sheet in which a circular hole has been cut with a saw. This simple process lends itself to a specific sequence. You could toss it together in a few ways, but logical progression through the following steps will guarantee a better result.

Make two identical domes and refine the edges by filing. Measure the diameter across the dome and set a dividers to exactly half this measurement: the radius of the circular shape of the dome. Strike a tiny dimple with a center punch in the middle of a sheet, then locate one leg of the dividers there and scribe an arc. This shows exactly where the dome will sit. Narrow the dividers slightly and use them to mark a concentric circle on the sheet. Drill a hole inside this line and use a saw to carefully cut out the inner circle, then smooth the cut edge with a half-round file.

The next step is to solder the dome onto the sheet, using the divider mark as a guide to where the dome will be centered over the hole. But wait. Anyone with some soldering experience knows that it's possible—no, probable—that

MAKING A DOMED LID

1 A dome is formed in a dapping block and filed to make a true edge. The sheet is drilled and sawn to make an interior hole.

2 Stitches are cut with a graver to hold the dome into place for soldering. These small fingers of metal will be cut away later.

3 The final lid after sawing off the excess sheet.

Joana Kao, *Really, Everything's Under Control.* Sterling, 22K, steel, brass, copper, glass, magnets, 1 1/4"Dia, photo: Doug Yaple. The box was fabricated from sheet and has magnets on both sides. These move the gears inside and also serve as the catch for the necklace.

the pieces will shift during soldering. It's therefore useful to learn a simple, effective way to lightly tack parts together for soldering.

Using Stitches

Stitches are sharp fingers of metal raised up out of the sheet with small steel chisels called *gravers.* Stitches are used to locate parts, to prevent elements from shifting during soldering, and to hold small units like hinge knuckles. In this case the dome needs to be precisely centered over the hole when it's soldered onto the sheet.

Sharpen a round or square (not flat) graver with a fine-grit whetstone or on fine sandpaper glued to a flat surface. Set the tip of the graver about 3 mm behind the scribed line and press it straight down into the metal. Slide the tool forward until it almost touches the line, making an effort to avoid scooping with the tip. Lift the handle of the graver to lever up the curl of metal just cut. If it's cut too shallow, the curl (or stitch) will be fragile; if the cut or lift is too forceful, it may break off. It's a good idea to practice on a piece of scrap to get the feel of the cut.

In these examples the rims have been thickened by adding material on the inside, but of course it's possible to work on the outside as well. Sometimes the thickening unit doubles as a surface decoration and molding. It's also worth repeating that a thicker rim means a stronger box or locket, and one with a longer life expectancy. Often, the area around a hinge is made thicker even if the rest of the rim is not. These supports are called *bearers,* and will be mentioned again in the next chapter of this book.

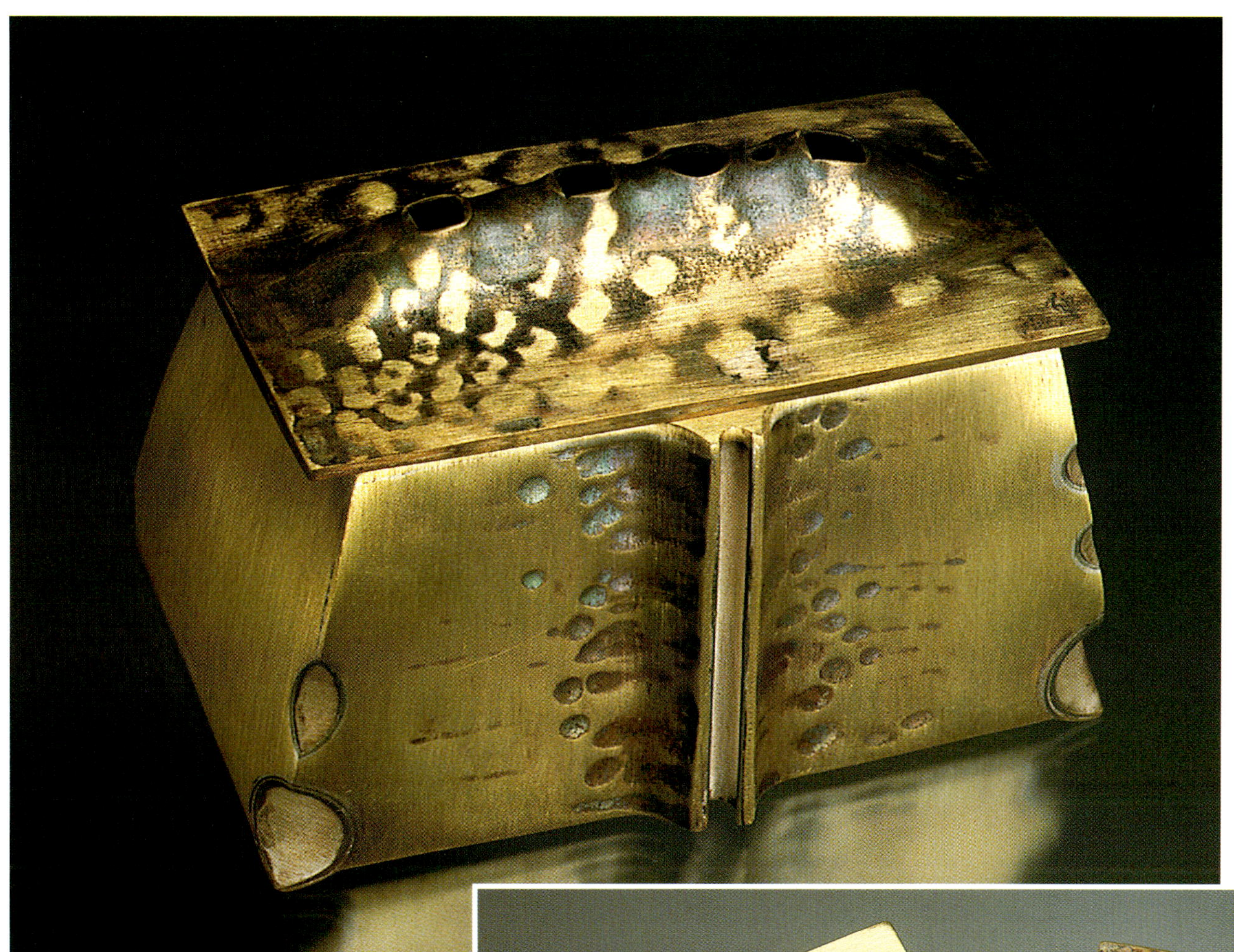

Tara Etheridge, box. Brass and silver, 3"W x 2"H x 2"D.

Hinges & Lids

This chapter describes a variety of hinges and lids, from simple to complex. Each design has its own reasons for being: each has a special look or feel, and many lend themselves to certain applications. Think of this chapter as a menu from which you can select the perfect hinge and lid for the box or locket you are making. As in the previous chapter on box construction, each example can be modified to yield a wide array of choices.

One of the pleasures of working in small-scale metal construction is the fusion of art and engineering. Nowhere is this more true than in box making, and especially in the construction of hinges.

As varied as hinges are, a few observations apply to all hinges used in small-scale metalwork. This is the "Because that's how it is..." list, the annoying rules that we'd like to ignore but can't. You might want to come back and reread it every once in a while.

Hinge Rules

1. A hinge must be straight.
2. Build it right rather than fix it later.
3. Close enough doesn't count.
4. Sequence is important.

Susan Bickford, *We Dreamt.* Sterling, copper, brass, 4"H x 1½"W x ¾"D.

1 **A hinge must be straight.** More specifically, the hinge pin, as well as the interior chamber of the hinge, must be straight as opposed to curved. The outside of a hinge can be sculpted to integrate with the curved contours of a form; this is familiar from compacts and watchcases. But the pin itself must be straight. If it isn't, the hinge will be tight and the pin will eventually break.

2 **Build it right rather than fix it later.** Though this advice makes sense in all fabrication, it has a specific meaning in the case of hinges.

Mariko Kusumoto, *Living Room* (interior). Sterling, nickel silver, wax, copper, found objects, 10½"H x 7½"W x 1"D, photos: M. Lee Fatherree.

Every box maker, at one time or another, has made a hinge that was *almost* perfect—perfect, except for that lump of solder where it shouldn't be or the tiny gap between components. In other aspects of fabrication, it's not uncommon to correct a small problem like this with a file or a bur. With hinges, that just won't work. The scale is so small and the tolerances so precise that even small problems can rarely be fixed in this way. More often, you'll waste time trying a half-dozen tools, mangle the hinge and get frustrated.

Get used to the idea of making it right, period. If the knuckles are too widely spaced, heat up the joint and push them closer together. If there is a lump of solder, heat up the area, dismantle the joint so you can clean it up, then put it back together.

3 Close enough doesn't count. Tolerances in a hinged construction are very tight because the arc of the swing magnifies any problem. Picture it this way: if you loosen the hinge on your front door and slide a folded paper under the hinge, it will affect the swing so much that the door will bump against the jamb on the side opposite the hinge. The thickness of a folded sheet of paper will throw the fit off by as much as a quarter inch!

In small metal boxes, a poor fit will show up in several ways. If a hinge is not perpendicular to the axis of the box, the lid will tilt to one side as the box or locket is opened. If the hinge is not properly seated against the bearers, there will be a gap between the box and lid. If there is space between the knuckles of a hinge—even a fraction of a millimeter—the hinge will feel loose and sloppy.

These close tolerances can seem like a huge frustration or a worthy challenge. They force you to pay attention, but reward your effort with the satisfaction of a demanding task done well.

4 Sequence is important. Again, this is generally true in metal fabrication, but particularly important with hinges. How many of us have assembled a box with easy solder, forgetting, in the focus of getting this job done, that we still have a hinge and clasp to construct?

Jiro J. Masuda, *Can You See Your Future With Her?* Sterling, 14K, mokumé, found object, 2" cube.

A Basic Hinge

Here it is, the white bread of hinges, the most common, most frequently used and simplest hinge. It has all the ingredients of every other hinge: tubular elements called *knuckles,* a well-prepared *seat* on which those knuckles rest, and a snug interior wire called a *hinge pin.* It's traditional for hinges to have an odd number of knuckles, with the greater number attached to the lower or larger piece.

Bearing Plates

It's probably obvious that a hinge is often placed under stress. Especially in the case of round or oval containers, where the hinge is tangent to the curve, it's often necessary to add additional support. When the material of the box is thin, the need becomes more apparent.

An extra piece of metal soldered onto the area of a hinge to reinforce it is called a *bearing plate* or *bearer.* By carrying the strain of the moving parts, it extends the life of the box, especially when the box is opened and closed frequently. For this reason, bearers are commonly

Tara Stephenson, *Narrow Focus #1.* Sterling, lens, mirror, 3"H x 2"W x 3"D.

MAKING THE BASIC HINGE

1 The hinge area is strengthened through the addition of a flat bar called a bearer. In this example, it's held for soldering with a clamp made from coat hanger wire.

2 Start the fitting process by filing a 45° angle on each edge of the hinge area. Make these planes flat, uniform and even.

3 Convert the V made by filing into a U that will perfectly match the contour of the tubing. Here a sawn-off nail is used to scrape away bits of silver to shape the groove on the closed box.

(continued on next page)

seen in snuff boxes, cigarette cases and matchsafes. Bearers are optional, but I've included one in this example to show how it fits into the assembly process.

Bearers can be cut from sheet stock or hammered from wire. This example uses 18-gauge sheet equal to the length of the box and $^{3}/_{16}$" wide. You'll need two pieces: one for the lid and another for the box. They are held into place with clips made of thick steel wire (e.g., coat hanger wire). Attach them to the box and lid with hard solder. After pickling and rinsing, file the edges flush.

Fitting the Knuckles

Before starting on the hinge, take a minute to sand the interface where the lid meets the box. This process is made easier if you have sheets of silicon carbide sandpaper glued to a flat tabletop or to sheets of Masonite or Plexiglas. True the metal edges with a file, then move through progressively finer papers until both edges are taken to their final finish. During later stages of construction, these areas will be much less accessible.

For a hinge to work properly, the knuckles (tube sections) must be in a straight line. The best way to achieve this is through careful preparation of the area that will hold the hinge—the seat, or *bearing*. The idea is to create a straight trough that has the same contour as the tubing and spans the box and lid. If the seat is correctly shaped, the rest of the process will go smoothly.

Start by filing a 45° slope on the edge of the box and again on the

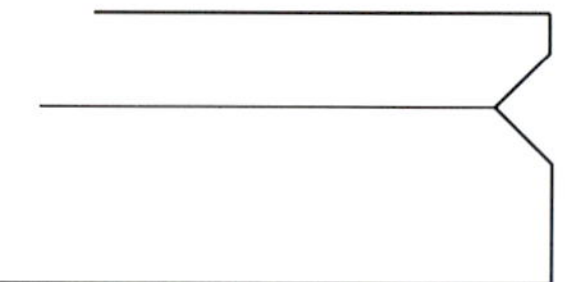

edge of the lid. Be sure they are straight, symmetrical and equal.

MAKING THE BASIC HINGE *(continued)*

4 A tube-cutting jig and knuckles. Note the way the fence is used to create multiple pieces of exactly the same length.

5 In a properly prepared groove, the knuckles have little choice except to lie smoothly in place.

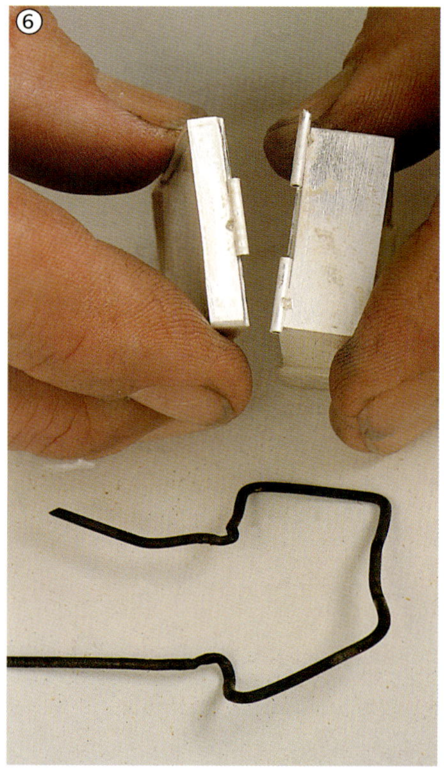

6 After quenching in water, remove the binding wire and carefully separate the pieces. Check to be certain the joints are strong and the placement correct.

J. Cummings, *Triptych Egg.* Sterling, wax candle, 7"H x 4"Dia, photos: M. Cavanaugh and K. Montague.

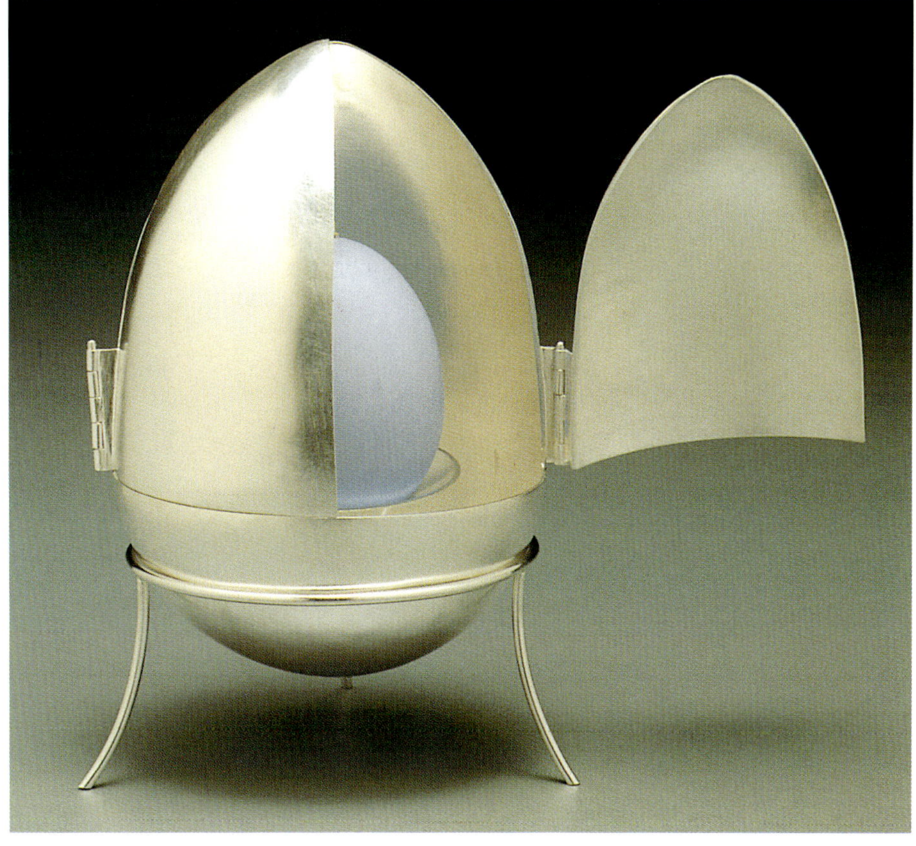

When the lid is in place on the box, the result is a 90° groove. At this point it's helpful to have the two parts firmly held together. Some people rely on their fingers, while others use tape, wire or glue. It's also possible to fill both box and lid with plaster or papier maché, then press the still-wet pieces together so they harden into a solid mass. This traditional method is very secure, but the hardened material must be removed by burning, soaking, or picking: a nuisance. Instead, I generally use a narrow strip of strong tape.

Making a U-Groove

Use a round file to convert the V-groove to a rounded U-groove. Because the diameter of a tapered file (the most common variety) increases along its length, a tapered file cannot make a perfect bearing.

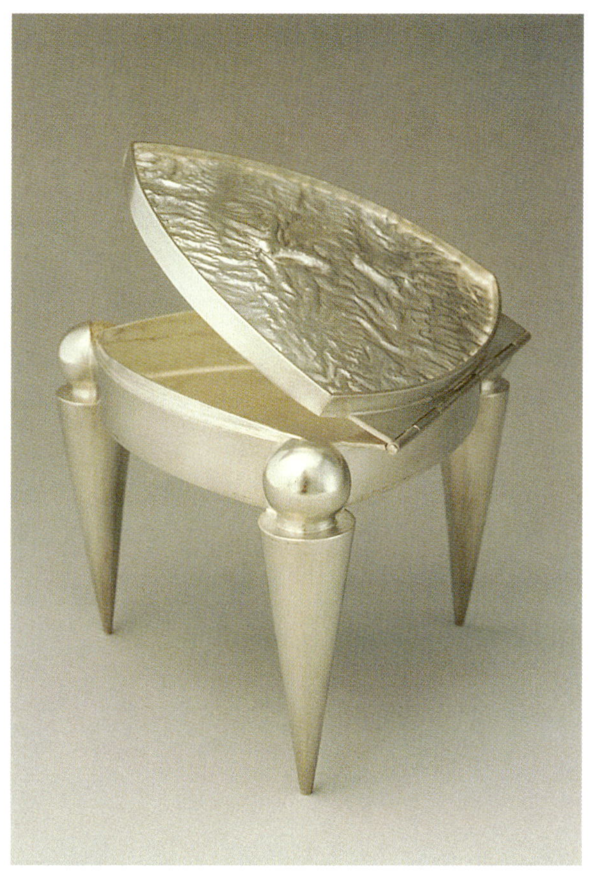

Above: Debbie LaFara, container. Sterling, reticulation silver, 3"H x 3½"Dia.

Left: Chris Irick, *Teetering on the Edge.* Sterling, copper, 4" cube. The train track pattern was photo-etched onto copper sheet; then the areas between the tracks were pierced with a saw. These pieces were fabricated into a box. The interior contains cast sterling train tracks.

Instead, look for a specialty tool called a *joint file,* which has a flat, smooth blade with rounded toothed edges. This is a watchmaker's tool, which means it's very small. You can also use a *parallel round file,* which has a cylindrical shape. Unfortunately, neither of these is commonly available; generally, you have to go to specialty tool suppliers. A more common alternative—available at hardware stores—is a $^{3}/_{16}$" round file made to resharpen the teeth of a chain saw; however, this will be too large for many projects.

Alternatively, find a nail with the same diameter as the hinge tubing. If what you have on hand is a little large, chuck it into a drill and run it against sandpaper to bring it down to size. To create a handle, either grip the nail in a pin vise or pound it into a section of dowel. Cut and file the end of the nail so it has a flat 90° end. Slide this along the groove to scrape away tiny slivers of metal, changing direction periodically until the tube lies snugly in place. It's amazing how quickly this simple tool will refine the seat.

Preparing the Knuckles

What's the right size for a hinge? This is primarily a matter of the look you want to create. Except for very tiny hinges—something under a millimeter in diameter—the strength of a hinge has more to do with the choice of material and the skill in construction than it does with size. Or, to say it another way, a hinge that is a quarter inch in diameter isn't necessarily stronger than a hinge half that size.

Before choosing tubing for a hinge, ask yourself about the effect you're seeking. Do you want the hinge to be obvious or hidden? Will an obvious hinge provide an interesting detail or will it break the flow of the form? Do you want the mystery of a hidden hinge, or something more prominent?

The process of making a hinge will automatically leave the metal fully annealed. And—by definition—these small bits of metal are going to take a lot of strain. It's important, therefore, to select a metal that will live up to its responsibility. Gold, for instance: 14K gold has all the properties needed for a strong hinge, but it's not always the right choice because of cost, color, etc. In the case of silver objects, use sterling—but because it's always softer than gold, use a slightly thicker gauge than you'd use for a 14K hinge of the same size. Nickel silver and bronze are preferred to brass, but again, use thick-walled tubes to compensate for their malleability. Copper is almost always a last choice, since it's so soft in its annealed state.

Measure the length of the hinge and divide this number into three, five or seven equal pieces. Cut sections of tubing slightly longer than this measurement. In the example shown, the width of the box is 25 mm, so I've made each of the three knuckles 9 mm long. This will allow the outer knuckles to project slightly past the box. The excess will be trimmed off after soldering.

In order for the hinge to operate smoothly and appear as a single unbroken line, it's important that the end of each tube be precisely square, i.e., perpendicular to the axis of the tube. This is harder than it might appear when cutting a tube freehand: the saw blade inevitably drifts sideways.

To correct for this, use a tube-cutting jig like the one shown on page 50. The tube is held in a V-groove while the saw blade slides between two hardened steel plates. The tool has the added advantage of an adjustable *fence,* a stopping plate that will hold a dimension from one cut to the next. These tools are somewhat expensive, but worth the investment if you'll be making many hinges.

The knuckles will be difficult to clean after they're cut, so get into the habit of rubbing the tube with Scotch-Brite or pumice before sawing off the pieces. Use the smallest saw blade you have to achieve the tidiest cut. If the sawing leaves a bur, remove it with a fine-toothed file and a light touch, so that you don't accidentally file a slope onto the squared end.

Steve A. Musselman, *Grid Box.* Sterling, copper, woven fine silver, enamel, 3"H x 3"Dia.

Attaching the Knuckles

Tie the box and lid together with steel binding wire, taking great care that the fit between the parts is exactly what you want. Cinch the binding wire in a Z-bend, as shown. That will allow the wire to relax as the box expands during heating.

Brent A. Williams, *Love, Dad,* reliquary box. Copper, bronze, brass, found objects, 3 3/8"H x 2 1/4"W x 3/4"D, photo: Robert Diamante.

Prop the box on a soldering block or in a bed of pumice so the prepared groove is horizontal. Apply a thin film of flux (too much will scatter the knuckles), and lay the short tubing pieces into position. Some sources suggest using a bit of steel wire as a pin to hold the knuckles in alignment. I don't recommend that step: the wire acts as a *heat-sink,* drawing heat from the torch. If the groove is properly prepared, there is no other place for the knuckles to sit but in perfect alignment.

Set a small piece of hard or medium solder onto each knuckle, bridging it to the box or lid alternately. Warm the piece slowly with a large bushy flame until the flux has completely dried, then concentrate on one side, either the box or the lid. Heat until the box approaches the flow point of the solder—that is, until a dull red color shows—then focus the torch flame briefly on each section of tubing. As soon as the solder starts to flow, pull the torch away.

When one side is done, move to the other. Repeat the process as before, focusing your attention first on the lid (or box), and then on each knuckle, one at a time. Heat only until the solder flows. The biggest danger is to linger on the joint, "just to make sure." In my experience, this is where I cause the hinge to seize up.

When you think the solder has flowed, even if you are a little uncertain about one or two places, remove the torch and quench the box

Mariko Kusumoto, *City, Living Room, Niwa* (covers). Sterling, copper, brass, nickel silver, found objects, all about $7^{1}/_{2}$"H x $5^{1}/_{4}$"W, photo: M. Lee Fatherree. "In order to suggest darkness and age, I use several different kinds of patinas. I think about where the found objects fit and how they interact with each other. Within the relatively small size of my works, I am striving to create a world of shadows, light, silence, spirituality and my personal memories."

in water. Hold it over the basin while you remove the binding wire, and open it. Check each knuckle by prying at it with your fingernail. Yes, this takes raw courage, but it's better to discover a weak joint now than later. If all the knuckles are solid, drop the work in a pickle bath to clean it up.

If a knuckle is loose, clean up the tube and use a file to selectively scrape the oxide off the area where the tubing will attach. The intent is to clean only the area where you want the solder to flow, leaving the rest of the hinge "dirty" (i.e., oxidized) to inhibit the flow. Re-tie the pieces together, reflux and place the tubing into position. The original solder is still in place, but solder is very loyal: once it fuses to a surface it prefers to stay there. For this reason, add a *small* piece of solder at the joint. It will fuse with the first batch and draw it into the joint. Repeat the heating as described above, breathe normally, and remain confident that the solder will do what you require of it.

After pickling and rinsing, slide a temporary pin through the hinge to test it. Use a round wire of any convenient metal, pulled to make it straight. Filing a point on the end is very helpful in feeding the hinge pin into position. If this is your first hinge, schedule about five minutes to open and close your box, smiling broadly.

Tara Stephenson, *Confidence, Security and Control.* Sterling, Plexiglas mirror, powder puff, 3"H x 2"W x $2\frac{1}{2}$"D.

Problems with Hinges

1. The knuckles are in alignment, but there are spaces between them.
2. The hinge pin won't go through the knuckles.
3. The hinge works well, but there is a gap between the box and the lid.

Kat Winters, *Sagemono Ensemble #2 Spider and Fly.* Sterling, copper, bronze, 4"H x 4"W x 1"D.

1 The knuckles are in alignment, but there are spaces between them. Reassemble the box and lid, reflux any knuckles that need to be moved, and heat the whole unit up to the flow point of the solder. Use a needle tool or sharp tweezers to tap the knuckles into position. In the case of a small box, secure the box with locking tweezers and a weight so you can slide the knuckles without having the box move across the soldering block.

If some of the knuckles are in the right place, insert a piece of binding wire, paper clip, straight pin, etc. into that section of the hinge. In this situation, the heat-sink phenomenon can work in your favor by causing these sections to achieve solder heat more slowly than the empty tubing.

2 The hinge pin won't go through the knuckles. In a perfect hinge, the pin comes through perfectly straight. If it doesn't go through on the first try, separate the box from the lid and slide the pin through the knuckles on only one unit, either the box or the lid. This will sometimes reveal the location of the problem. It's often possible to bend a knuckle back into place. With a metal hinge pin in the tube, grip the knuckle with flat-nose pliers and rotate it very slightly. Repeat the test until the hinge pin slides unassisted through all the sections.

If the pin won't go through at all, it's possible that a piece of solder has flowed into the tube. This is unlikely if you used an appropriately small amount of solder. More often the blockage will be caused by flux residue. Phew! Set the work back into fresh hot pickle and give it time—perhaps half an hour—to dissolve the block.

If the tube is blocked with solder, it's usually possible to drill it out, assuming you have a drill bit equal to the inside diameter of the tube. Sometimes it's more efficient to lift off the blocked tube and replace it with a new one.

3 The hinge works well, but there is a gap between the box and the lid. First, be certain the temporary hinge pin you are using is the correct size. (Test pins don't usually need to be a tight fit, but don't try to correct this problem unless the pin fills the interior of the hinge completely.)

Next, cut a piece of matchbook cardboard (or fold a piece of paper) to make a strip a little longer than the box and about 1/4" wide. Slide this into the box very close to the hinge, making certain that it's in contact with each side. Press the box closed, hard. This will put stress on the hinge, pulling the knuckles apart slightly. Remove the paper and test the box. If the gap remains, try again—perhaps with another layer of cardboard to increase leverage.

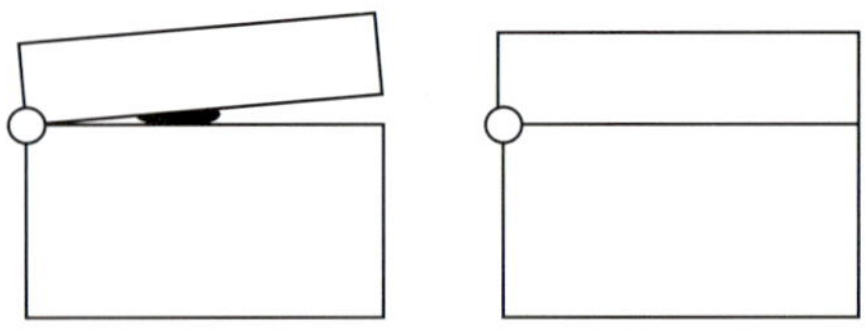

Flush Hinge

This hinge has a significantly different appearance than the basic hinge, but its construction is almost identical. The construction sequence is the same as just described, but the tubing used for the knuckles is thicker than normal. Thick-walled tube is available from some suppliers, but because it's not a common item you should be prepared to make your own.

Making Thick-Walled Tubing

You'll need a large drawplate and either a strong back or a *drawbench*. The latter is a piece of equipment designed to increase leverage when pulling wire or tubing through a drawplate. Traditionally it consists of a flat bed with a vise at one end to hold the drawplate. A large wheel at the other end is attached to a belt or chain. The sample is inserted so its tapered tip extends through a hole in the plate where it can be grasped in *draw tongs*—a kind of strong pliers—that can be attached to the belt (shown below).

Start with purchased tubing or tubing you've made yourself (see Chapter 4, "Basics and Practices"). If you've made the tubing yourself, be certain the seam is completely soldered along its length. The drawing process will make the tube smaller as it thickens the wall, so you'll need to start with an oversized tube.

To provide a grip for the draw tongs, solder a piece of wire into the tube so it projects out about an inch. Any sort of wire will do; brass or nickel silver is typically used because of the low cost. File a taper on this wire and blend its contour into the tube as shown. This is the leading edge that will extend through the drawplate. When drawing is complete, the end section will be cut off and discarded.

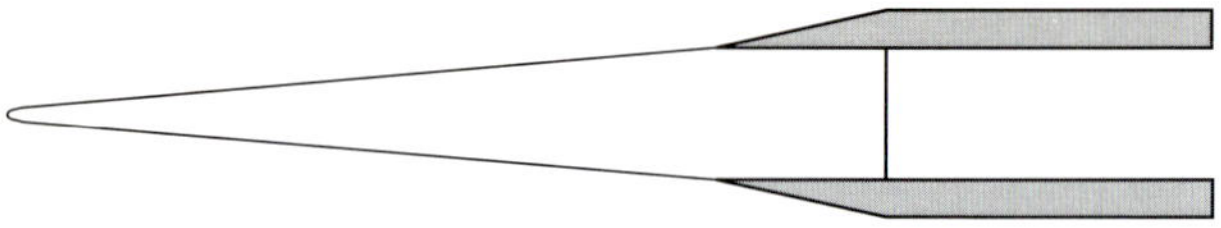

MAKING A FLUSH HINGE

1 A length of base metal wire is soldered into a tube to provide a grip for the drawing process. Tubing is drawn exactly like wire, either freehand or with a drawbench.

2 File and drill a bearing the same size as the tubing to be used for the hinge. In this case the groove is "buried" lower in the box.

3 Thick-walled tubes are soldered into place exactly as in the earlier hinge. After filing and sanding, the knuckle will almost disappear.

Jan Baum, *Varying Direction #2*, pendant locket. Sterling, steel, nickel silver, 2"H x 1$^{1}/_{4}$"W x 1$^{1}/_{2}$"D, photo: Phil Harris.

When it's important to bring the inside diameter to a specific size (and this is not always the case), you will need to have on hand a steel, nickel or brass wire of that dimension. Cut a piece several inches longer than the tube, coat it with oil or Vaseline, and slide it into the tube for the drawing process. When the tube comes down to the point where it lies against this core, the metal will stop thickening the wall and extend itself in length instead. To remove the wire, hold the tube against the front of the drawplate so that only the interior core wire projects out. Pull to withdraw the wire.

The Hinge Seat

Make a seat for the hinge as described in the directions for the basic hinge, using files and scrapers. It's almost always necessary to use a bearing plate when making a flush hinge, because it's critical to have a large mass of metal adjacent to the hinge. Create a seat that allows the knuckles to be recessed to two-thirds of their depth. In the ideal arrangement, the cradle matches the contour of the tubing perfectly. To make this "wraparound" seat, start with a small V-groove, then bind the lid and box together and drill it from the side with a bit that perfectly matches the tubing.

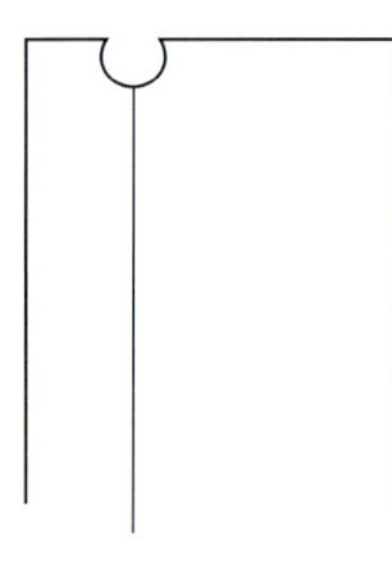

Position and solder the hinge components exactly as in the basic hinge. So that the flush hinge will "disappear," it's important that the solder fill all gaps—but don't be fooled into thinking the way to achieve this is by using more solder. Instead, take special care that the knuckles fit tightly into their seat. If this is difficult, solder the knuckles in place, pickle the work, and burnish the area around the knuckles to bring the seat to the hinge. Reflux and heat the piece again (this time the lid and the box can be kept separated) until the solder reflows and fills all the spaces.

Spacing the Knuckles

This hinge can be used to show a neat trick intended to guarantee spacing between knuckles. It's a clever idea that can be used in a variety of settings. Start with a tube equal to the entire length of the hinge. Mark the locations of the knuckles: in this case that means dividing the tube into equal thirds. With a small saw blade, cut three-fourths of the way through the tube at each line, then turn the saw 90°

and cut away most of the center knuckle. This will leave a bridge of metal that holds the first and third knuckle in alignment and perfectly spaced. When soldering the tube into the box, be certain the bridge is rotated as far from the box as possible so it can be easily cut away.

When the box and lid are in final assembly, file away the third of the hinge that stands up above the box. At this stage it's easy to see why the tube must be inset deeper than halfway. Complete the job with a sequence of sandpaper, and finish by buffing with a leather-coated buffing stick.

Cradle Hinge

The cradle hinge is named for the applied bearing that holds or "cradles" the knuckles. It's especially useful on round objects, like the locket shown on pages 62 and 63, since it provides support where the curve of the object would otherwise allow little contact for a conventional hinge.

Make or purchase tubing and cut a piece a little longer than the

length of the intended hinge. This will be the cradle. The initial length of the cradle is not critical because any excess can be trimmed off later in the process. What *is* important is that the tubing be well soldered and straight.

Cut a piece of the same tubing and draw it down until it slides smoothly (i.e., telescopes) into the first tube. If the holes in your drawplate do not provide exactly the right size, it might be necessary to sand the outside of the tube. This is the tubing from which the knuckles will be cut.

As with the basic hinge, filing a bearing is a very important part of the process of making a cradle hinge. If the seat is straight, correctly sized and properly placed, all subsequent steps will be easy and look good. This is as true of the cradle hinge as any other.

File a 45° facet on both the lid and the box, then bind the pieces together with tape, glue or wire. File the groove until it perfectly matches the cradle. At this step you'll be converting a V-groove into a U-groove. Use round files and a scraper made from a common nail as described in the last section. This is quicker in the telling than at the bench, but take your time and do it right.

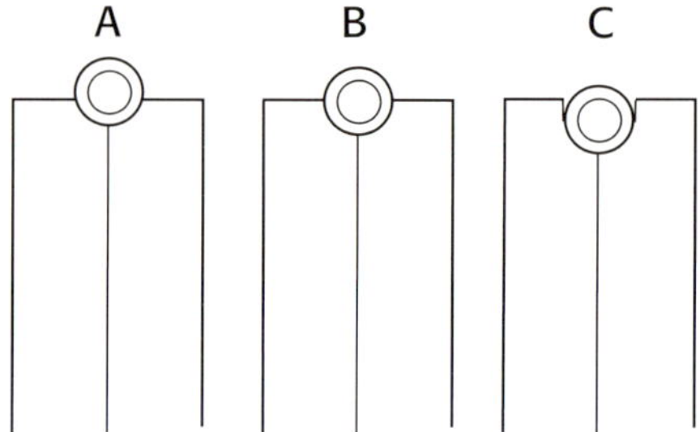

Continue until the cradle (the larger-diameter tubing) fits into the groove snugly. The drawing shows three possible depths, each of which is acceptable. Anything less integrated than **A** risks an insecure joint because there is limited contact. Setting the hinge deeper than **C** will create a hinge that cannot open wide enough for you to see the inside of the locket.

To prepare the locket for soldering, remove any tape, papier maché or glue that was used to hold it together, and tie the pieces with binding wire. Wrap the wire loosely and twist the ends to close it. Then make a Z-bend with flat-nose pliers to cinch it tight.

Creating the Cradle

With a large or medium saw blade, cut a slot along the long axis of the cradle tubing. Go all the way through, but only on one side—don't cut the tube into two pieces! Clean the tube with Scotch-Brite, coat it with flux, and lay it into the bearing groove so the cut is pointing directly down. In other words, line up the open slot with the interface of the locket halves. Seen from the end and imagining a clock face, you've positioned the groove at six o'clock. Place pieces of hard solder on the outside of the cradle on both sides and solder the cradle, attaching it to both pieces. Quench in water.

Examine the cradle area closely to be sure the joint is sound. Pull the locket open very slightly—just enough to ensure that the box and lid have not been soldered together. Do this over the water dish, because the box will be full from the quench. As you'll see in a moment, the beauty of this system is that the cradle you've just attached is a perfect fit with the knuckles. If you force the locket open at this stage you'll bend the cradle tube and destroy the fit. Proceed gently!

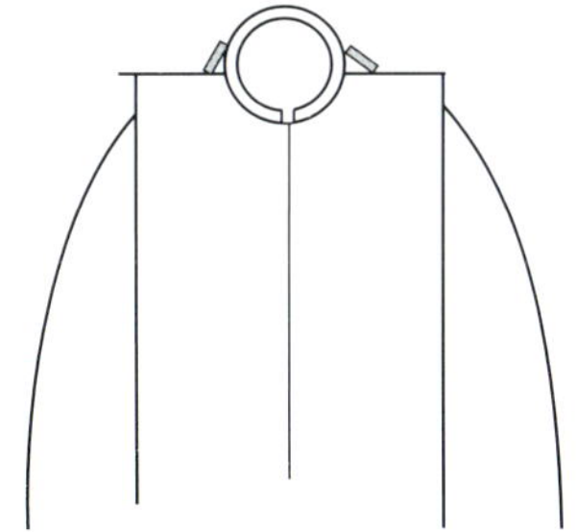

If the pieces don't move, flux glass may be locking them together. Drop the piece in pickle and cross your fingers. If that doesn't do it—i.e., if you've accidentally soldered the halves together—heat the pieces and gingerly pull them apart, then go back a few steps and try again.

Above:
Lee Graham,
compass.
Sterling,
2 1/4"Dia.

Right:
Hinge detail.

Assuming that all is well, use a saw to cut along the length of the cradle, making the cut about a third of the way around the tube from the first slot. Looking at the end of the cradle tube and imagining a clock face again, if the first cut was at six o'clock, make this cut around ten. This will allow the box to separate from the lid. One unit will have a large section of cradle and the other will have a smaller piece. Now, cut off and discard a tiny section (one-third) of the larger cradle tube so the two units are identical.

Look at what you've done! On both the box and the lid, you've made bearings that are:

- perfectly parallel to each other;
- a perfect fit with the knuckles;
- perfectly positioned.

Attaching the Knuckles

Cut three pieces of the inner tubing, each equal to a third of the total length of the hinge. Examine the ends of each knuckle to be certain there are no burs left from the cutting; file lightly if necessary.

Set a cleaned and fluxed knuckle into the center of the lid cradle and lay a tiny piece of medium solder so it touches the tube and cradle. Because the cradle extends out from the piece, it's usually pretty easy to bring the hinge area to soldering temperature. Don't make the piece so hot the cradle itself comes loose. After soldering, clean the piece in pickle.

Hold the box and lid together and make scribe marks on the cradle section attached to the box so you'll know where to solder the outer knuckles. Use a small triangular file to make these marks more visible—you'll need to see them while soldering.

Flux the cradle and set the two knuckles in place so the space between them just matches the length of the center tube. You can hold the lid in position to check this. Put solder chips in place as before, and heat slowly to prevent the pieces from moving.

MAKING A CRADLE HINGE

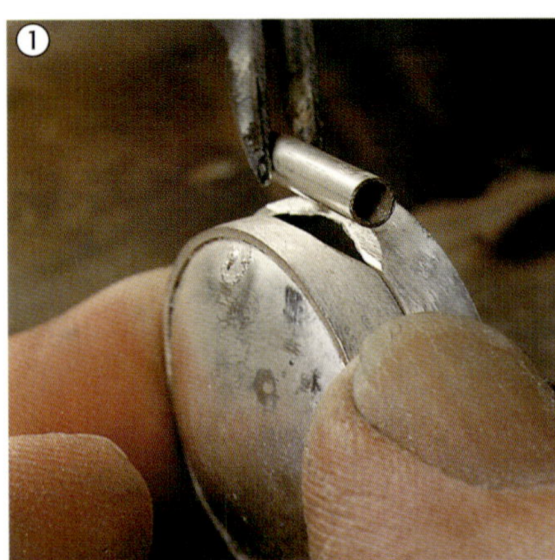

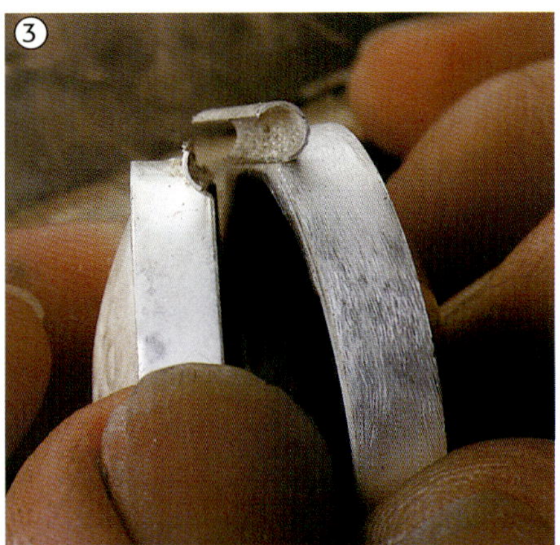

1 Prepare the locket to receive the cradle (the outer tube of the pair). As before, care at this stage will make the process both neater and easier.

2 Saw a slot in the cradle tube and position it onto the locket with the slot facing down. Lay a piece of solder on each side.

3 When the cradle tube is attached, cut the pieces apart, leaving one-third of the tube on one side and two-thirds on the other.

4 Place a knuckle into the center of one of the cradles and solder it with a tiny chip of solder.

5 Mark the location of the outer knuckles with small notches filed into the top of the cradle. Unlike pencil or ink markings, these will show up throughout the firing.

6 The finished cradle hinge is both elegant and practical. The cradle increases the strength of the hinge and creates a stop that controls the arc of opening.

When the solder flows, but before quenching, test the two pieces against each other. Because one unit is still hot, the test is approximate, but it will show if the gap is too large or too small. In either case, the only solution is to reheat the locket and slide one of the knuckles to correct the problem. Grip the work in cross-lock tweezers to anchor it as you do this. The maneuver is delicate, but not as difficult as you might think. Double-check the spacing, heave a sigh of relief, and pickle the pieces.

After rinsing, test the hinge by inserting a temporary pin. Notice that the cradle, in addition to adding strength to the box, pro-

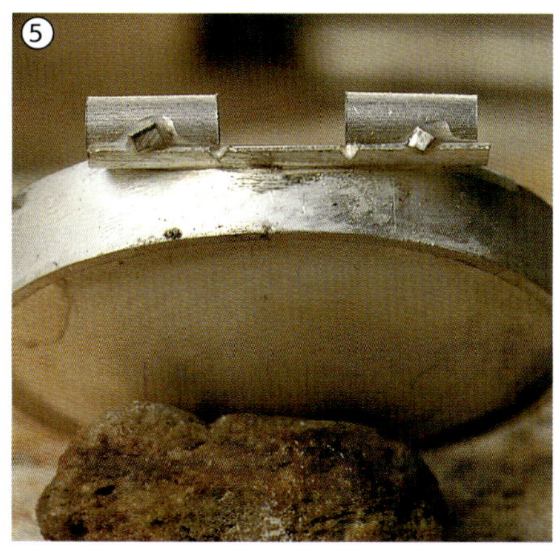

Chris Irick, *A Means of Escape.* Sterling, copper, brass, 1 1/2"Dia. This locket is worn as a watch chain. The outer case was die-formed and constructed; the inner section, a receding spiral staircase, was cast in sterling and soldered into the piece.

Rachel Alvarez, locket.
Sterling, brass screen,
1"H x 1"W x 1"D,
photos: Robert Diamante.

vides a stop as the lid is opened. This is the result of the one-third section of cradle that was removed—the less taken, the shallower the arc of opening. To allow the box to open further, slide a flat file along the edges of the cradle. Test frequently as you fine-tune this dimension.

Side Walls as Hinges

The hinge described below is an example of a different way to think about hinges, a way that might suggest other innovative solutions.

Basic Method

In the example pictured below, the walls of the box serve as what might be considered the outer knuckles of the hinge. A panel of metal that fits neatly inside the box is cut and filed with a bevel on the end that will take the hinge. Cut a piece of tubing a little longer than the width of the panel; the extra length is useful in case the tubing shifts slightly during soldering. File an angled facet along the axis of the tube to ensure a solid joint.

After soldering and pickling, the excess tubing is filed away, and the joint is sanded into a seamless construction.

Solderless Method

In situations where soldering is not possible or desired, a different kind of hinge can be made by rolling the lid material around a rod. If the lid is thick, hammer or roll the end to make it thinner. The portion that is used for the knuckle will need to be three times the diameter of the hinge pin. Use pliers to curl the end of the panel.

Set the panel upside down on a soft surface like a sandbag, rubber mat or pile of newspapers. Set a steel rod (e.g., a nail) about the same size as the desired hinge pin onto the panel and strike it with a hammer. Complete the curling with a forming tool you can easily make yourself from a finger-length section of wooden dowel. Drill a hole through the dowel, using a bit slightly larger than the diameter of the hinge pin. Cut off enough of the dowel to leave exactly half of the drilled hole. Tap this over the curl to complete the bend.

Vise Method

Start with a panel that is longer than the box, perhaps by as much as half its length. Fold the sheet over and insert a steel hinge pin. Clamp the assembly tightly in a large vise, using cardboard to protect the surface. Close the vise while pressing down on the unit to keep the bend close to the rod. Strike the bend area sideways with a mallet to push the bend so it's not centered on the panel. The flap can be riveted if desired, or cut away entirely with a saw or separating disk.

SIDE WALL HINGES

1 Prepare the tube by filing a flat facet along its length. This will make a stronger joint.

2 Thin the end of the lid by hammering or rolling. Anneal it, then bend it over with pliers. You can refine the curve with a simple tool made from a dowel as described above.

3 Use a vise to roll a piece of sheet onto a rod to make a knuckle. This is a coarse solution, but it has the advantage of using no heat. In some cases, as when working with painted tin, it works especially well.

4 Drill holes in the side walls of the box and slide a pin through the lid knuckle.

Ned Foulkrod, *Post Mortem Box.* Sterling, bronze, 14K, amethyst, 1¾"H x 3"W x 2¼"D. The box is constructed from fused sterling and 14K gold with an amethyst in a prong setting. The interior is cast bronze.

Drilling the Box

Regardless of the method used to make the long center knuckle, the lid should be set into position and sighted to determine the location of the holes in the walls of the box. Mark, centerpunch and drill, using a bit that is slightly smaller than the pin: this allows for small adjustments in case the holes are not perfectly located. Use a round needle file or a tapered steel bur to enlarge the holes. It may also be necessary to file the end of the box to allow the hinge to rotate smoothly.

At the opposite end, use a flat file to cut away enough of the wall so the lid can lie flush. In some cases you might allow a small overhang for lifting the lid.

Lori Talcott, *Bird.*
Sterling, brass,
3½"H x 2"W,
photos: Richard
Nicol.

Finger Hinge

Like the preceding example, this hinge uses sheet metal rather than tubing to make the knuckles. It's a little more difficult to make than a tubing hinge, but its rarity makes it special. Simply stated, the idea is to construct a hinge of panels of thick sheet that are standing on edge. The trick is to ensure the correct spacing between the panels and a hole that runs directly through the entire assembly. There are many ways to achieve this: the following example should provide some food for thought.

Sequence

It often happens that the workings of a hinge are located inside a box where they are difficult to see, much less construct. While that's not always the case with this particular hinge, it does offer an opportunity to learn how to tackle that problem. You'll be making the lid and completing the hinge before attaching it to the box.

Make a long rectangular box by following the method described in the first example of Chapter 1. After making the walls, cut out the floor panel and temporarily insert it to hold the box in shape, but don't solder it in place. Next, cut out a panel exactly the correct width to fit into the box, but at least a half inch longer than the box. Mark the place where the lid should hinge, use a square to scribe a perpendicular line at that point, and cut the panel into two pieces. The larger piece is the lid; the other, which will be fixed to the box, we'll call the "attached element."

The Hinge Segments

In this box, the knuckles will be made from 14-gauge sheet sterling that has been sawn into strips about 1/4" wide. In the end, the hinge will consist of five square

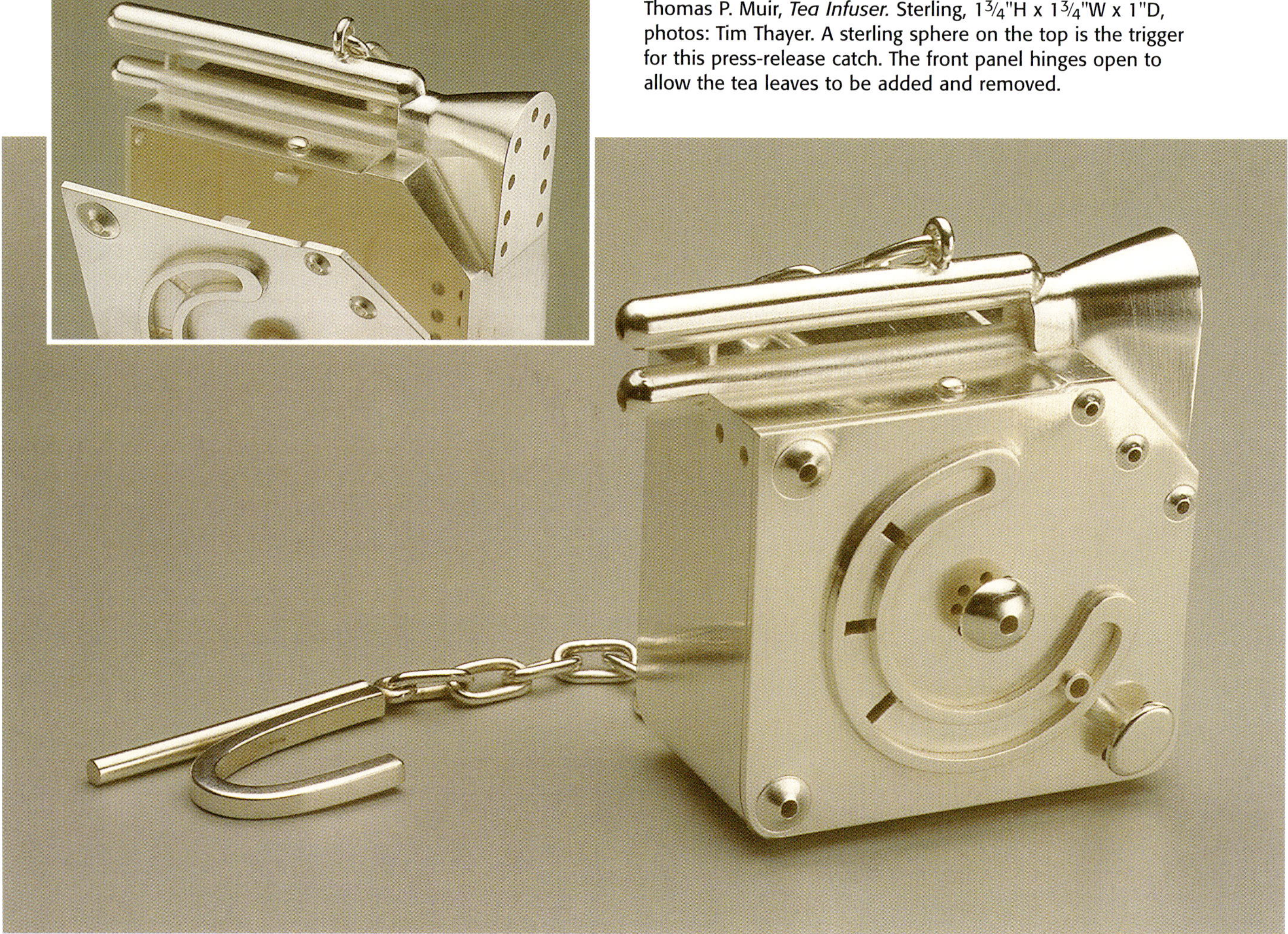

Thomas P. Muir, *Tea Infuser.* Sterling, 1 3/4"H x 1 3/4"W x 1"D, photos: Tim Thayer. A sterling sphere on the top is the trigger for this press-release catch. The front panel hinges open to allow the tea leaves to be added and removed.

panels of sheet standing parallel and evenly spaced. The trick will be to devise a system that will hold each of the pieces in just the right location for soldering.

Start by bending a one-inch strip in half as if you were folding a paper in two. Lay a piece of the 14-gauge sheet in the fold to create the exact gap, and press the fold closed with pliers or in a small vise. The result is a U in which the space between the vertical arms is exactly 14-gauge. The curved part will be cut away later.

To make the three-knuckle element, start by soldering a half-inch strip of sheet in the center of a longer piece to make a T with a very long top. Bend as described above, again using spacers of 14-gauge sheet to determine the gap. This is the piece being sawn in the first photo below.

File the edges of both units and check to be certain all edges are flat and square. Remove burs with a flat needle file in preparation for soldering.

The box walls are made from sterling sheet; a bottom is cut and fitted so it snaps into place. This is then set aside until later in the process. Bands of thick silver sheet have been bent into shapes that will temporarily hold the pieces parallel and the correct distance apart.

Attaching the Knuckles

Working on what will be the underside of the lid, mark the centerline. This is most easily done by setting the dividers to a spacing that is, by eye, a little larger than half the width. With one leg overhanging the panel on the left, scribe a short line. Then, with one leg overhanging the right side, repeat the process—the result is two lines that indicate the center of the sheet.

Apply a film of flux, and center the three-knuckle unit so its edge

MAKING A FINGER HINGE

1 After the hinge units are soldered onto the lid pieces, the surrounding sheet is cut away.

2 Careful sawing is important to create a hinge that moves smoothly.

3 Use files to trim the pieces, checking often so you don't take away too much.

4 Hold the lid together and drill through the five panels.

David Jones, *Fritz and His Horse*, box. Sterling, 24K, fine silver, copper, brass, 1945 PEP pin, antique mother-of-pearl buttons, 9"H x 8"W x 7"D, photo: Tom Mills.
"When I'm making a piece I seem to be transported into this kind of zone. When I am in the 'zone' it's kind of like a tornado at the bench, tools flying, metal dropping, little conversation except talking to myself."

is even with the edge of the panel. Lay a snippet of solder at each end of each piece, and heat until the solder flows. Rinse, pickle and dry.

Use a saw to cut away the sheet metal between each of the three knuckles, leaving the area on either side of the outer knuckles untouched. Use a flat needle file to smooth the area around the knuckles, taking pains to keep all edges truly vertical. Pay special attention to the inner edges of the two rectangles just cut away to be certain they are in a straight line.

Set the lid, still upside-down, onto the shorter panel (the top). With a needle or similar sharp tool, scribe the area just sawn out, leaving its outline on the unit that will be attached to the box. This will indicate the placement of the other set of knuckles. Solder them down as just described. After pickling and rinsing, saw out the area between the knuckles.

Lay a straightedge across the bottom of the slots just cut and scribe a faint line. Saw along this to remove the sections on either side of the hinge. I prefer to cut a little outside the line so I can fine-tune the fit by filing.

Slide the hinge halves together and trial fit a wire through the holes. They'll probably line up—but not perfectly. Because the original hole was intentionally undersized, you can now use a slightly larger drill bit to go through the entire hinge. Take pains to keep the bit parallel with the plane of the lid.

If all has gone well, the two parts, lid and top, will fit together so snugly that the line between them will almost disappear—and the hinge won't open at all! To allow clearance for the rotation, it's necessary to file away a small

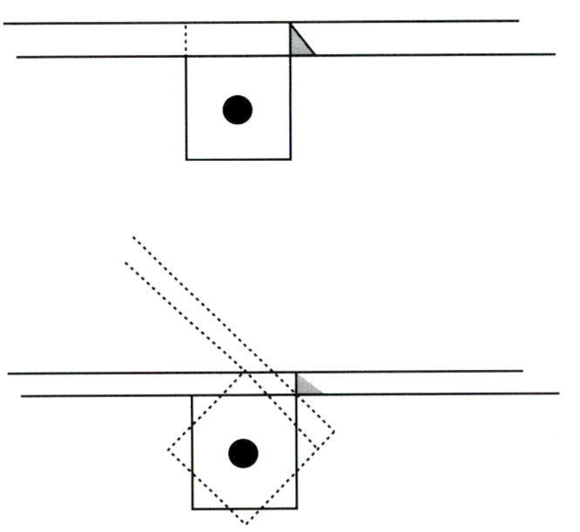

amount of metal (shaded areas in the drawing) from the underside of the top where the tips of the knuckles are binding up. Go slowly, taking away as little as possible to allow the mechanism to work.

Assembling the Box

Cut a tab into the other end of the box to provide a handle by which the lid can be lifted. This can be as wide or narrow as your design sense indicates. After you have made the tab, mark the outline on the rim of the box and cut or file it away, as shown below. This can serve as the catch for the box; simply make the fit so tight it clicks when engaged.

It will now be possible to lay the two pieces upside-down on the bench and set the walls of the box onto them. The point is to determine exactly where to cut the top so it fits snugly into the walls. Scribe a line, cut with a saw, and

ASSEMBLING THE FINGER HINGE BOX

1 When the hinge is working smoothly, rivet the hinge and solder this panel of the lid into the box.

2 Saw or file a notch across the front of the box to catch a tab on the lid.

3 The bottom panel is inserted into the box and soldered in place.

4 The finished box with a five-knuckle interior hinge.

file until this unit fits neatly into place. At this point, the hinge can be completed with a final pin which is riveted to hold it into the box. Because it won't show, it's also possible to simply bend the pin at each end. Solder the top to the walls of the box. Insert the floor, solder it in place and the box is complete.

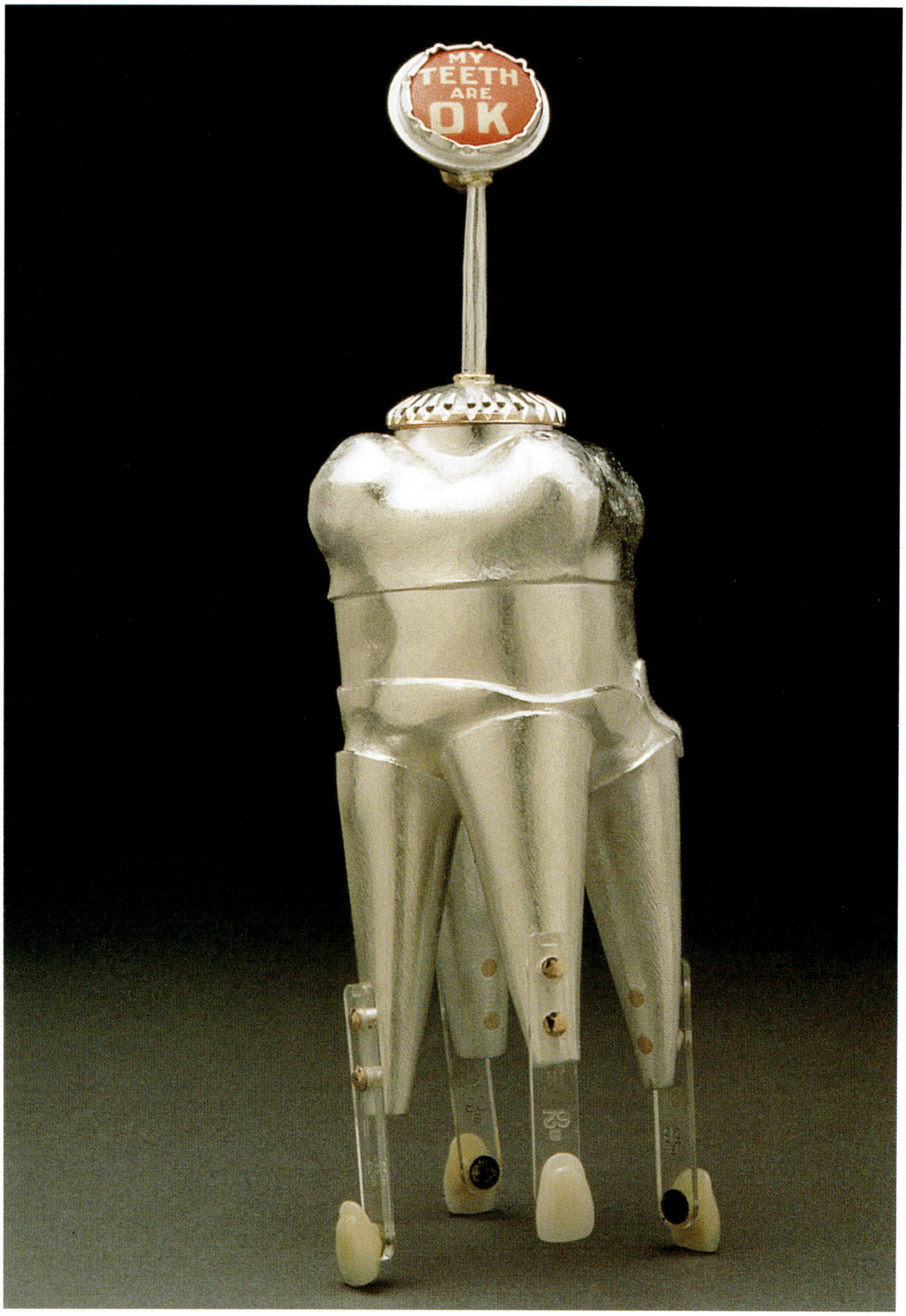

David Jones, *My Teeth Are OK*, box. Sterling, copper, 18K, fine silver, antique badge, dental tooth samples, 22K tooth cap, 9"H x 3½"W x 3½"D, photo: Tom Mills. "I consider myself a three-dimensional animator fascinated with the figure, both animal and human ... I do not sketch pieces beforehand—they just seem to go directly from my brain to an object."

Stand-Away Hinges

All of the hinges described so far operate close to the point where the lid meets the box. When the container is open, the lid seems to touch the box at the hinge. This section describes an alternative in which the lid lifts up and away from the box. Though not widely used in traditional metalwork, this category of hinge offers a wide range of opportunity. For examples, look at the hinges in kitchen cupboards and automobile trunks and hoods.

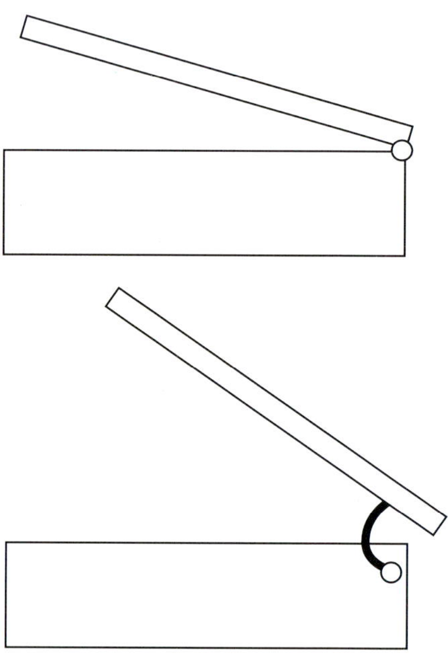

The uses of a stand-away hinge are both practical and aesthetic. A familiar example is the gas-fill door on a car. In almost every case the door sits flush with the lines of the car, held by an invisible hinge. The effect is sophisticated and unobtrusive. The practical advantage of this system is that the door moves out of the way to allow better access to the filling tube of the gas tank.

Concept

The idea of a stand-away hinge is really very simple. The hinge itself is nothing more than a conventional arrangement of knuckles. They can be made from tubing or sheet, odd-numbered or even, large or small. The knuckles on at least one element (the lid or the box) are not connected directly but are attached instead with an extension. Depending on its location, this has the effect of lifting the lid either up and away or to the side as it opens.

Construction

In many ways, stand-away hinges are about the easiest to make. The "extender"—that is, the curved metal piece that bridges the knuckle and the lid—can usually be bent after the hinge is made, to fine-tune the fitting. This is a luxury not available with a conventional hinge, where the parts must be precisely located before soldering.

The example shown here uses a particular sequence for a stand-away hinge; other designs determine their own needs. In the example, the hinge is hidden inside the box. The project shows a hexagonal box, but almost any shape can accommodate this hinge.

The first step is to make the bottom and lid of the box. Cut, clean and file the parts to create their final shape, then sand through the usual sequence to a medium-grit paper. Final finishing is left until after all soldering is complete.

Drill through the box to attach the outer knuckles. Because this hinge takes up space inside the box, it's usually located near an edge. I prefer to drill holes a bit smaller than I need, then enlarge them with careful use of a needle file. A piece of tubing must slide easily through the holes without bending. With the tube sticking out slightly on each side, solder it in place. If the box will be subject to heavy use, it's possible to solder in

Chris Irick, *Egress.* Copper, brass, sterling, herculoy, 21"H x 1¾"W x 1¼"D.

MAKING A STAND-AWAY HINGE

1 Drill holes in the walls of the box and slide a tube through. Solder it into place. The center section is then cut away with a separating disk. Notice the curved bridge element; it's soldered to a tube that will become the center knuckle.

2 The center knuckle is set in place and the hinge is temporarily assembled. The bridge is cut to the correct length.

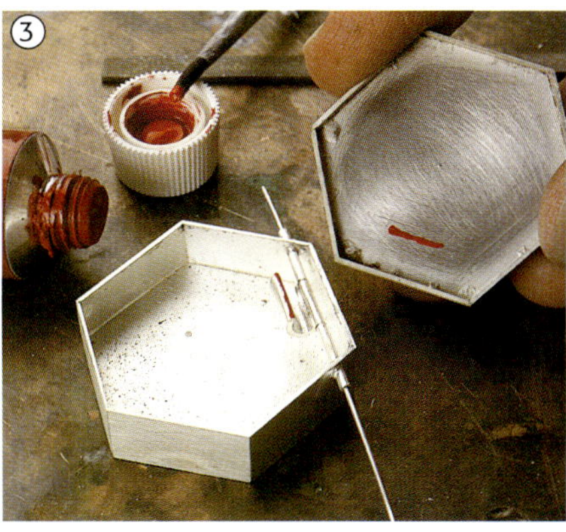

3 A drop of paint is applied to the top of the bridge, then the lid is carefully lowered into place. This leaves a stripe of paint on the inside of the lid that shows where to solder the bridge. Use a scribe to scratch lines around this stripe; the paint will quickly burn away. *(continued on next page)*

additional support—either sheet or wire—though this is usually unnecessary.

Cut away the middle section of the tube to make a space for the center knuckle. This can be done with a file, a saw or a separating disk—or perhaps a combination of several tools. If the hinge is difficult to reach, use this alternative method. Cut the tube sections before soldering them in place. Then hold them in alignment with a temporary hinge pin of pencil lead or steel binding wire (both materials that cannot be accidentally soldered into the tube). This rod must be a good fit so the tube sections are held in perfect alignment.

Next, cut a piece of the same tubing to the same length as the space just made, and file the ends square and neat. Solder it onto a strip of sheet or pieces of wire or bar, as shown in the example. The action will be the same, so the choice here has to do with design and the materials available. After pickling and rinsing, bend the connecting bridge slightly and hold the hinge and lid in place so that you can visualize what will happen as the box opens and closes.

Cut the connector to what seems like the correct size and attach it temporarily to the inside of the lid with wax or hot glue. The variables here are the location of the joint, and the length and curve of the connector. With the piece in your hands you'll be able to experiment to determine what changes are necessary to make the hinge operate smoothly.

A One-Use Jig

Once you've made final adjustments, all that remains is to replace the temporary wax joint with a soldered one. Ah, but how to hold the proper angle while dismantling and reassembling the piece? Here's a suggestion: make a one-use jig from a piece of scrap metal, as shown. This can be as simple as a measuring device that records the angle (in which case you solder freehand and bend the piece to the

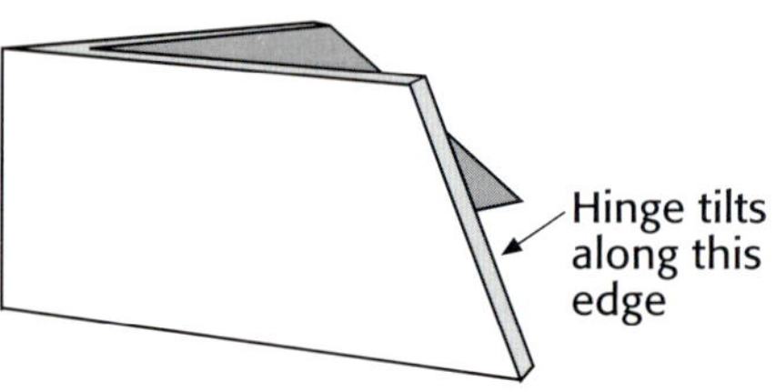

MAKING A STAND-AWAY HINGE *(continued)*

4 A simple jig can be used to hold the center knuckle at the correct angle for soldering. Jigs like this are invented and made as needed for special soldering requirements.

5 The assembled box. Notice how the hinge lifts the lid up and away from the box.

Jan Harrell, *River Oaks Baptist Box.* Sterling, enamel, 4"Dia. This is one of a series of boxes made for a fund-raising auction at the artist's daughter's school. The names of all the members of the class were etched into the sterling container. The name of the school was incorporated into the enameled lid. A container seems a fitting metaphor for education and the well-defined period of time we spend in our academic years.

precise angle later), or it can include tabs that will hold the pieces for soldering. When the joint is complete, the tabs are bent back, the jig is pulled off and the piece is in place. A similar result can be achieved by cutting a wedge from firebrick and using it, perhaps aided by straight pins, to secure the pieces for soldering

Clean the pieces in preparation for final assembly. Trial fit the lid and bend the connector as needed to allow the lid to close neatly. Insert a hinge pin of the same metal of which the box is made, snip and rivet the ends, and burnish them flush with the surface so they almost disappear.

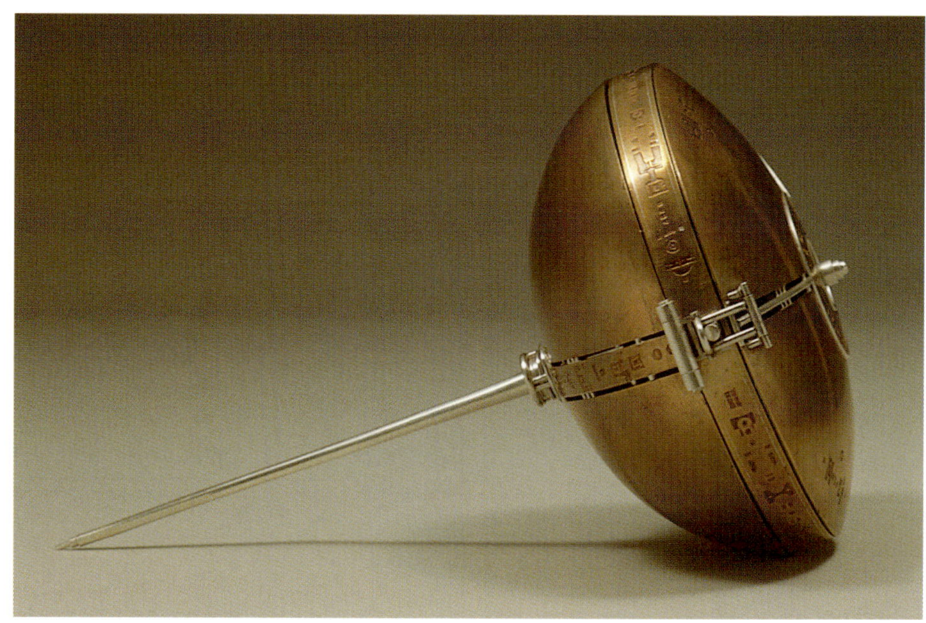

This page and facing page: Cappy Counard Wolf, *Mississippi Pearl Box.* Sterling, brass, pearls, 7"H x 4"D. "Ultimately, the viewer will find that this box holds pearls within its depths, but its purpose is more about the act of exploring its many puzzle-like layers."

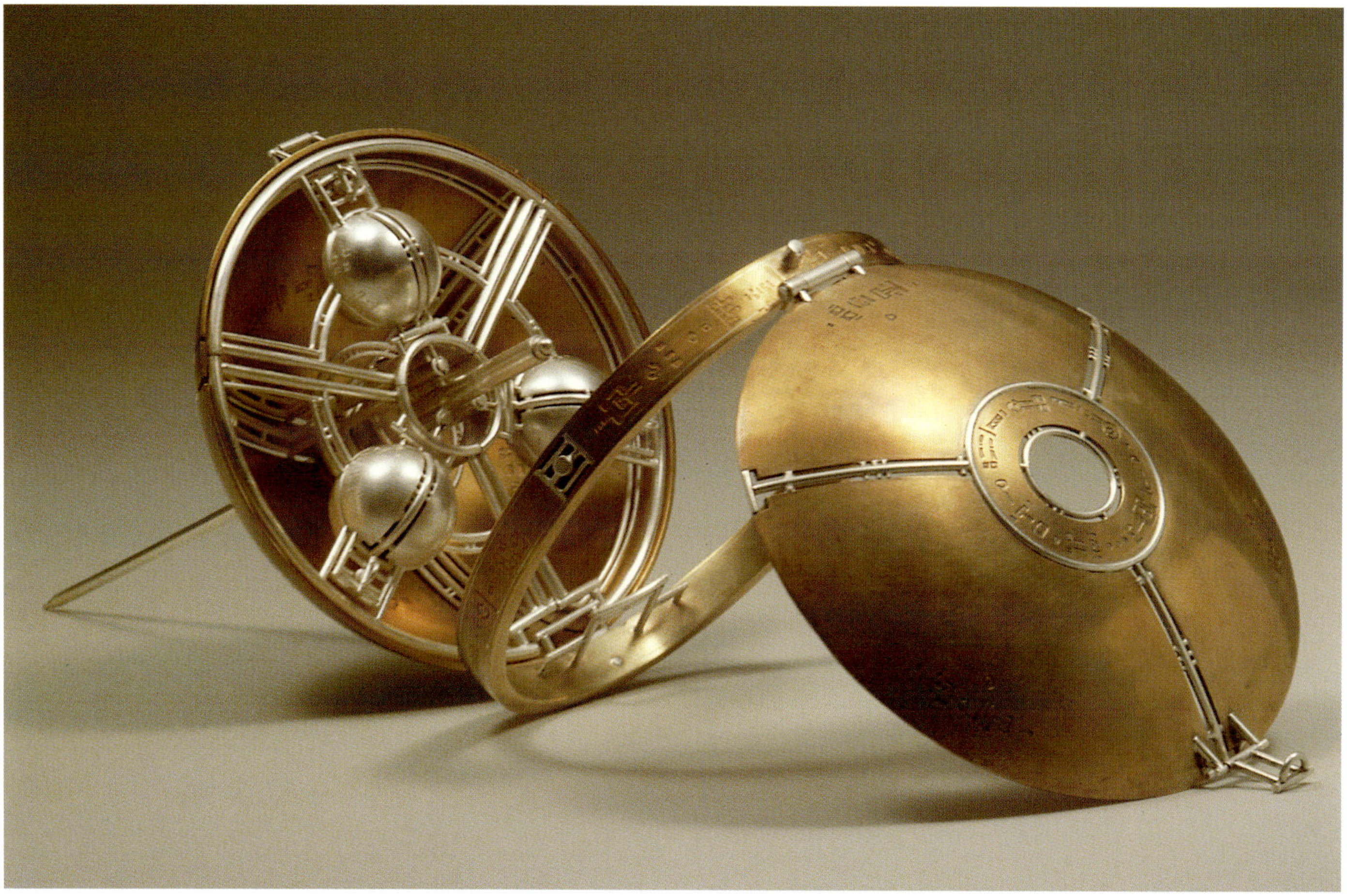

External Springs

The spring-loaded hinges described in this section might just as easily fall under the heading of "catches," because they can be used to hold a box or locket closed. Beyond that, spring-loaded hinges give a sense of life and excitement to a box, as with the classic jack-in-the-box.

The spring in this first example is external to the hinge itself, and is generally—though not always—visible. In most cases the hinge is constructed slightly differently to accommodate the spring, but some external springs can be added to a conventional hinge arrangement. The internal springs in the next section are hidden and always involve construction unique to the hinge.

Materials

Keep in mind that some metals are springier than others, and that all springy metals can be made "more springy" or "less springy," depending on their treatment. Making a spring, then, is a simple matter of selecting the correct material and handling it in the ideal way.

The most springy metal available is properly hardened and tempered steel, followed in progression by platinum, titanium, 14K white gold, 14K yellow gold, nickel silver, brass, silver solder and sterling. In every case, work-hardened metal has more bounce than annealed metal. The essence of working with springs lies in understanding these properties and devising ways to make use of them.

In some cases, it's difficult to contrive a way to attach a hardened piece of steel without annealing, which will remove the springiness. In those cases it might be better to substitute another metal. There are also cases in which the cost of one metal is prohibitive so a method is devised that allows the use of a cheaper alternative. This is the confluence of engineering, materials science and innovation. Rise to the occasion!

Sources of Spring Steel

One source for spring steel is in household objects that are made of, well, spring steel. Safety pins are probably the best source, followed closely by paper clips and hairpins. These can be used with their temper (springiness) intact, or they can be annealed, shaped and retempered. This process is explained below.

Spring steel is also available as piano wire, sold through some tool catalogs and often available from piano repair shops. Most hardware stores sell replacement coil springs. If they don't have the size you need, it's often possible to re-

Lilyana Bekic, *TV Snax*, candy jar. Anodized aluminum, sterling, found objects, 5½"H x 9"W x 4⅛"D.

work an existing spring. Watch and clock mainsprings are an excellent source of spring steel, but do not remove these yourself! The springs are razor-like ribbons of metal under extreme tension. Watch and clock technicians use special tools designed to ease the tension in a spring so it can be safely removed. Without this tool, it's very dangerous to remove a spring from its casing.

In this and all the following examples, it will be helpful to understand the general concept more than the specific action. When I'm designing a spring-loaded device, the conversation that goes on in my head is embarrassingly simple. I start by reminding myself that the spring has a position it *wants* to be in. Set a spring on the table and look at it—that's it: the "rest position." Loading a spring is nothing more than bending it out of this position and giving it the chance to return. The idea is to make this return action do what you want, like open the lid. Keep this in mind in the following examples and you will soon be able to go beyond the spring hinges shown here to invent your own.

Coil Spring

A coil spring is made by wrapping a wire around a rod, a process that resembles the first step in making jump rings. Anyone who has done this has noticed that after winding, the wire springs back (or unwinds) a little bit. The tougher or springier the wire, the more it unwinds.

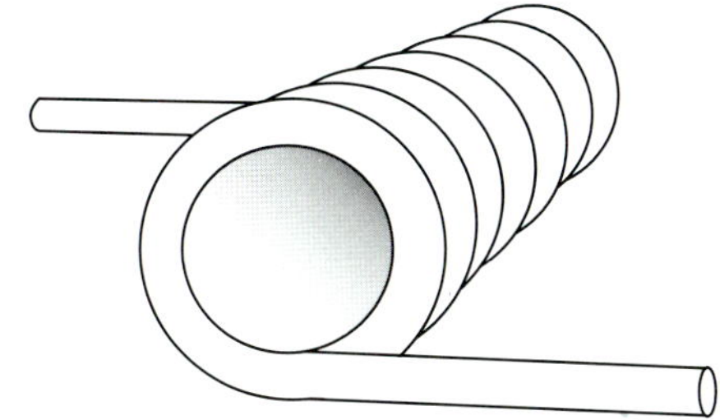

This springiness is captured in the "legs" of the spring, the ends that are left projecting out from the coil. Again, it's useful to recall the position of the spring at rest: what does it want to do? In the drawing below, the version on the left illustrates the spring at rest and the version on the right shows the box closed. The arrows show how the force of the spring will work.

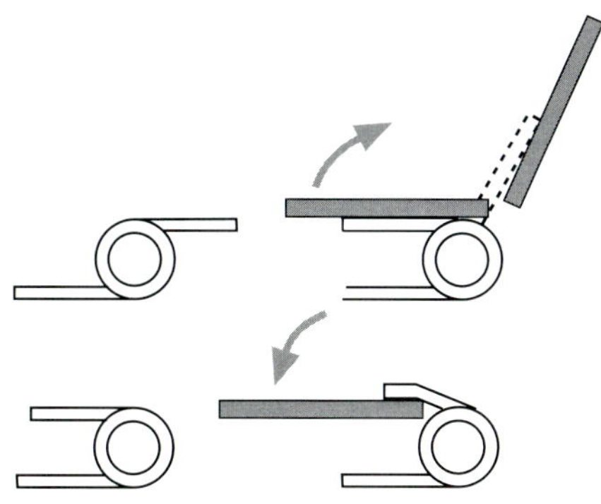

Construction

This familiar spring hinge can be used in many situations. Make a hinge in any of the usual ways, but allow a space for the spring to be located between two knuckles. The knuckles soldered on can be made

LOADING A COIL SPRING

1 The knuckles for this box were made from coils of brass wire. This makes an interesting detail, and also helps camouflage the coil spring that is located between the knuckles.

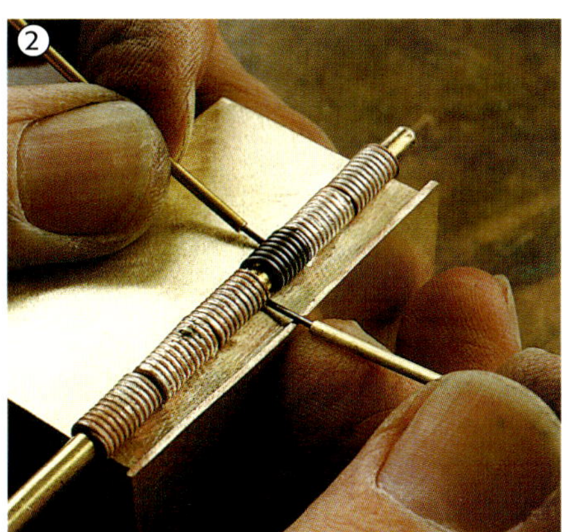

2 Use a small piece of tubing as a temporary handle to help load the spring. This is a tricky job at best, made easier with the help of an extra pair of hands.

3 The spring in this box holds the lid closed, so it could almost be called the catch.

Rachel Alverez, locket. Sterling, $1\frac{1}{2}$"W, photo: Robert Diamante.

of tubing, sheet, or, as in the photos on page 79, of wire wound onto a rod and soldered. The latter has the advantage of disguising the spring.

When the lid is being assembled onto the box, insert the spring so that the hinge pin passes through it. If the legs of the spring are left "at rest," the spring has no effect. To load the spring, the legs must be engaged, or hooked around the lid and box in a way that either pulls the lid open or makes it want to snap shut. The spring for these opposite configurations is the same; what differs is where the legs are held in tension.

Loading a spring is a clumsy affair at best and usually easier with an extra pair of hands. Leaving the legs of the spring long can be helpful, but they sometimes get in the way or are difficult to trim down later. I use two small pieces of tubing as temporary handles that can be slipped over the ends of the

Alan Perry, *Browsing Through Time.*
Bronze, found objects, 1"H x 2"W x 4$\frac{1}{2}$"D,
photos: Robert Diamante.
The etchings are two maps of the Christian Shore neighborhood in Portsmouth, New Hampshire, and include the artist's house. Opening the box takes the viewer back in time from the 1879 map to an 1813 version. The boxes contain objects found on the shoreline of the mapped area.

spring to facilitate bending them into place.

With the spring in place, rotate the legs as desired so the lid will snap closed or be thrown open. In the latter case, a catch will be needed. Slide a hinge pin through the tubing and spring, and check the action. If everything works as it should, tap the ends of the hinge pin to form a rivet head.

Leaf Spring

A leaf spring is a curved bar of tempered metal. In this example, it's used to pop a box open slightly, a stereotypical gesture we associate with a railroad conductor looking at his pocket watch. This action keeps the catch under slight tension, an effect that makes the catch more secure.

The size is determined by the weight of the load it must lift. In this example, the lid is small and the desired action is a gentle opening, so the spring can be delicate.

The drawing shows the action of the spring, a simple vertical post that is pressed down (like a tall man under a low ceiling) when the box is closed. Given the chance (i.e., when the catch is released) the spring will stand up straight, pushing the lid as it does so.

In order to preserve the temper of the spring, it must be held into the box by a cold connection. This could be by rivets, tabs, staples, screws or any of several other devices. This example uses the easiest solution I know: simple friction.

Use a hard-drawn wire, in this case, hard silver solder. This alloy has high tensile strength and comes from the refiner as a very springy coil. A round wire has an equal tendency to bend in any direction, so start by planishing the end flat. This will allow you to "steer" the direction of the bend, making the wire go where you want it to go. Flatten a section roughly equal to the height of the box.

Bend a right angle at the base of the planishing and bend a form that, when collapsed, will fit snugly around the bottom interior of the box. This is not complicated, but requires some patient fitting. The idea is to snap the wire into the box so that it blends in and is secure. The vertical post is curved slightly inward and the top is curled so it will not jam against the lid as the box is closed. A few trials will demonstrate what bending and trimming are needed to make the spring do its job.

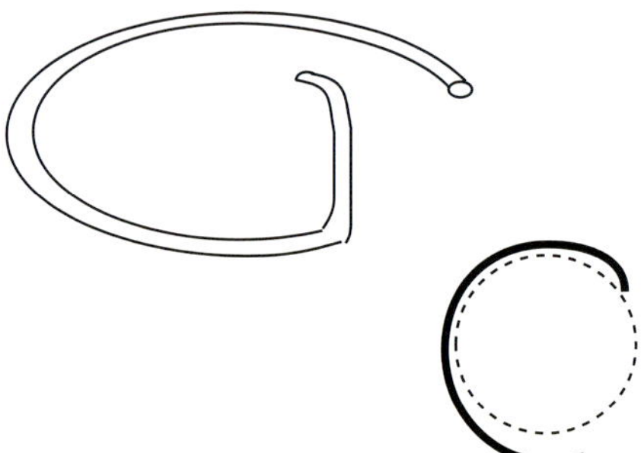

Side-Mounted Leaf Spring

In this variation of the device described above, a hardened spring is mounted on the inside wall of a box. In the photograph below, it's shown popping the lid open, but it could be used to lift a panel, to eject a figure, or to release a hidden catch. For more about these devices, see the information on trick catches at the end of the Chapter 3.

In this example, the spring is

This cutaway view shows the interior of a box in which a side-mounted leaf spring is used to lift the lid. The spring is held in place with rivets.

Jeff Wise, *Contained Kiva,* locket broach. 18K, coral, opal, 2½"Dia, photo: Paul Ambrose. This wearable container is based on an architectural form used by Native American tribes. The knot element rotates on a rivet and is attached on the inside to a hook. Turning the knot 90° releases the hook.

made of sheet metal, though it could as easily have been made of wire. Here, it allows a piece to be fitted into the interior corner of the box. The spring is planished to flatten and work-harden it, bent so it will be under tension when the box is closed, then riveted into the box. It would be possible to solder a pad into the lid to make a surface for the spring to ride against. This might be necessary, for instance, in the case of a lid with uneven contours.

Internal Springs

In this variation, an unconventional hinge pin is used to build tension into the hinge. It can be used to make the box fly open or snap shut.

Construction

This hinge is appropriate for many kinds of boxes, but it will work best

INTERNAL SPRING WEDGES

1 Small wedges are made by filing the end of a wire to the shape shown. The file marks are left to provide a little "tooth" to hold the wedges into place.

2 One of the wedge shapes is left attached to its wire, making it easier to handle. The spring, held in pliers, is rotated a turn or two and then the short wedge is pressed in to lock the spring in place.

Dominique Giordano, pin/pendant. Sterling silver, colored epoxy inlay, 20" x 1" x 2$^{1}/_{4}$", photo: Ralph Gabriner.

if the hinge is at least an inch long and can be made of tubing with an inside diameter of no less than 1 mm. Though the hinge can be made of any metal, the knuckles in this hinge are under slightly more pressure than with normal hinges. If a weak metal is used (copper, for instance), it should be made thick enough to compensate.

The hinge is conventional except that it contains an even number of knuckles. This will guarantee that the end knuckles are not attached to the same unit. In other words, if the knuckle on one end is attached to the lid, the knuckle at the other end will be attached to the box. As usual, complete the fabrication, finishing and patina of the box before assembling the hinge.

In this case, the hinge pin will be made of two or three thin springy strips of metal. For best re-

Rachel Alvarez, locket. Copper, 1¾"Dia, photo: Robert Diamante.

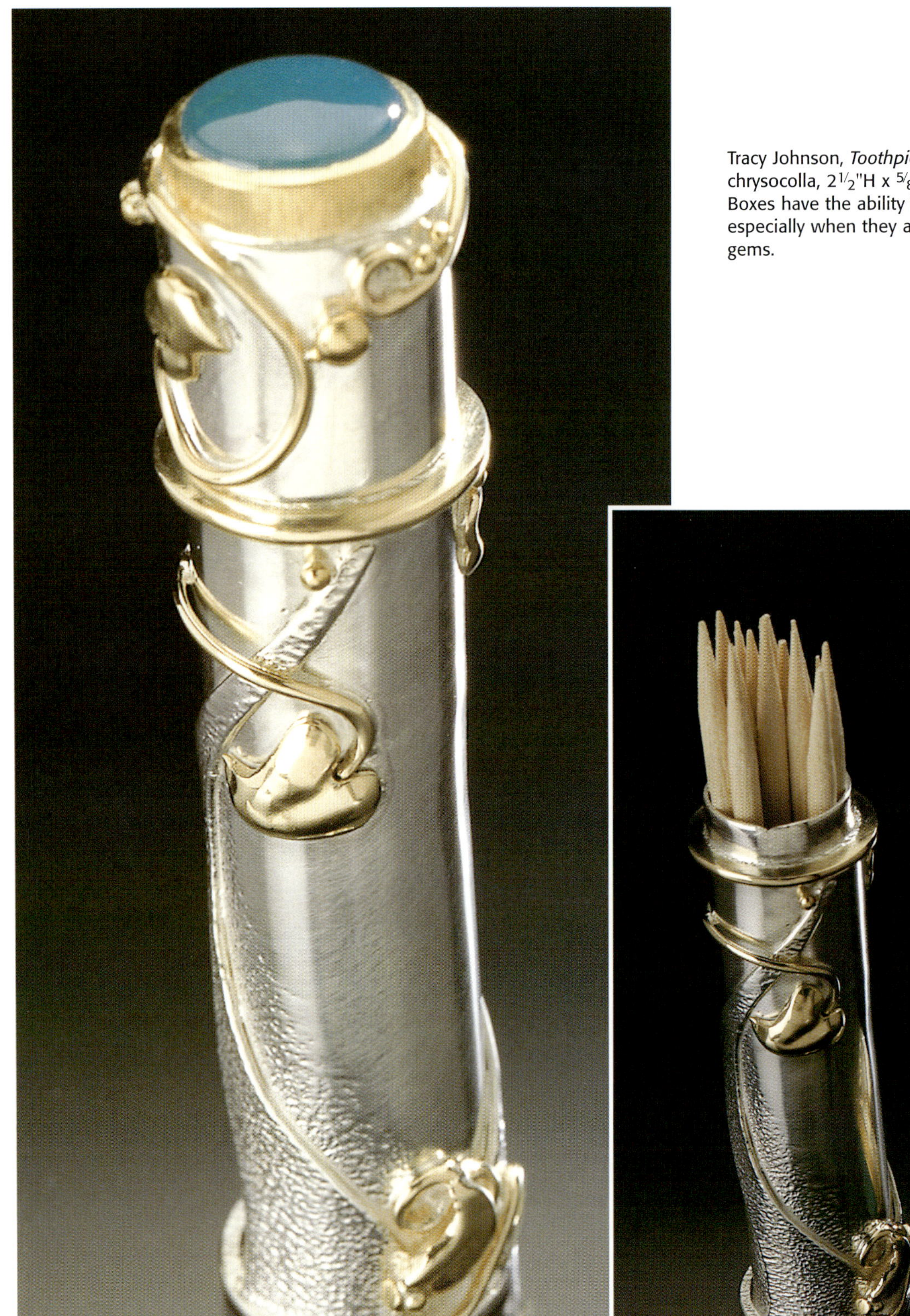

Tracy Johnson, *Toothpick Holder.* Sterling, 14K, chrysocolla, $2\frac{1}{2}$"H x $\frac{5}{8}$"Dia, photos: Robert Diamante. Boxes have the ability to make everyday objects special, especially when they are made of precious metals and gems.

Elizabeth Bone, boxes. Sterling, 18K, 2"H x 1 1/4"Dia.

sults use spring steel; alternatives include hard-drawn brass, nickel silver, platinum, or silver solder. Cut strips at least an inch longer than the length of the hinge and make certain that they fit easily through the knuckles. If the strips are slightly too wide, they can be made narrower by filing, grinding or sanding.

The springiness of this hinge depends on keeping the hinge pin attached to the end knuckles. This must be done without heat, which would anneal the spring and defeat the purpose. We'll do it here through friction, with wedges filed from wire of the same metal as the hinge (in this example, sterling). The wedges are tapered and filed flat on one surface, like a doorstop wedge. We will need four of them.

Finishing the Hinge

To load the hinge, set the box and lid together and slide the springy strips through the tubing, allowing the spring to project out slightly. Secure them at one end by sliding two wedges into place, one above and one below the strips. Cut off the wedges (if necessary) so they are the same length as each other. Tap them snugly into the tube with a small hammer. To ensure longevity you might even add a tiny drop of epoxy on the wedges, though this spring was used effectively long before modern adhesives were invented.

The springy strips will be sticking out the other end of the hinge. Grasp them at their tip with pliers and give the wire a half turn. Slide a wedge into position to temporarily lock the spring into the end knuckle. This will make it possible to determine whether you twisted the wire in the correct direction. Test the lid gently to see whether it wants to spring open or wants to spring closed. If it doesn't do what *you* want, remove the wedge and rotate the wires in the opposite direction.

When you have determined the correct rotation, slide the wedges into place, pressing each one firmly. Again, a small amount of adhesive can be used on the wedge to anchor it into the tube. The wedges are then tapped into place with a small hammer or a hammer and punch. Trim away the excess metal on both the wedges and the spring, and complete the hinge by filing and sanding both ends.

Lids Without Hinges

Not every box needs to open like a clamshell, two more or less identical units joined by a hinge. One option, a lid that lifts off entirely, has already been described. Here are a couple of other styles:

Making Tracks for a Sliding Lid

Fabricating tracks is an exciting challenge for a box maker. To operate smoothly, the tracks need to be straight, uniform and precisely measured. These factors are easy to control when milling a slot with a cutting machine, but challenging to construct from parts. Although the following section shows a general method, each project will dictate its specific needs. Use the following example as a guide, but feel free to tailor the process to your own requirements. The specific sizes given here are for the benefit of description only—alter the dimensions to be in proportion with your box.

Frame Method

For this example, I've made two identical, tightly fitted frames and soldered them as completed units into a previously made box. The lid can then slide between them.

In this case I've chosen to make the track from 14-gauge (1.6 mm) square wire, but other sizes and shapes can be used. It's critical that the wire be perfectly straight. Sight along the wire to locate any irregularities, then use your fingers to straighten the bends. Follow the procedure that was used to make the walls of the box: file a V-groove

Ken Cory, *Cupcake Box.* Copper, sterling, 3"Dia, photo: Lynn Thompson. The icing lifts off as the lid.

into a length of wire to create an L equivalent to a long and short side of the box. Repeat this four times (i.e., make four L's). You are now prepared to make the two identical rectangular frames that will become the top and bottom of the track. Solder the scored and bent corners to strengthen them.

Take careful measurements from the box. (I'm assuming here that the box itself is symmetrical and that all corners are exactly 90°. If this is not the case, you'll have to custom make the frame so it fits.) Cut one of the shorter legs so it measures exactly the inside width of the box, less the dimension of the square wire you are using. To determine this, set a piece of the wire into the box, lay one of the L-shaped pieces against it and scribe a mark where the frame meets the corner. Cut, file and double-check. When you're certain it's accurate, cut the three other short legs to the same length.

Repeat the process with the longer legs of the frame pieces, this time taking a measure across the front of the box. The goal is to create frame components that will fit snugly into the inside of the box. With the pieces carefully measured and cut as described, the frames can be soldered into their complete form with confidence that they will be the correct size. Minor filing and a slight rounding of the corners might be necessary to make the frames fit snugly into the box.

Attaching the Frames

The next step is to solder the first frame into position to become the lower edge of the track. Can you depend on the tension of a good fit to hold it in place while it's being

USING THE FRAME METHOD

1 Frames of square wire are made as the first step for a sliding lid. The frames are made just the right size to fit snugly into the box.

2 Use scraps of copper or brass to hold the frames in position for soldering. If the strips are cut to the correct height, the frames cannot accidentally fall during soldering.

3 A similar trick is used to ensure spacing between the lower and upper frames. Pieces of pencil lead are laid on the first frame, then the second one is pressed uniformly against it.

4 The finished box.

soldered? Well, maybe. This is a little risky because the box will expand slightly when heated and, at a

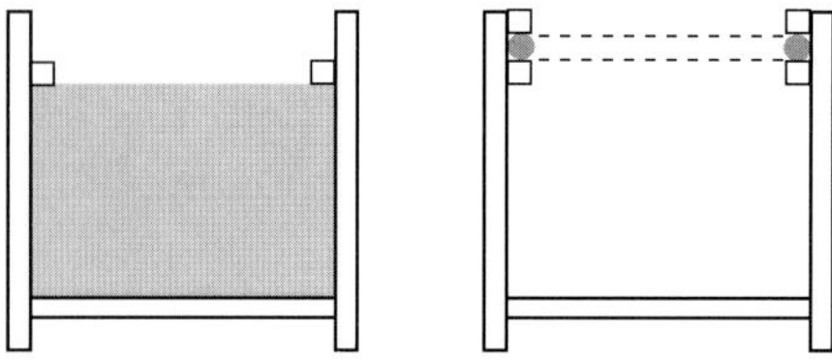

critical moment, the frame may tilt. Here's a simple way to avoid the problem.

Determine the correct height from the floor of the box to the bottom edge of the frame and cut thin sheets of copper or brass to exactly this height. Bend these strips into zigzags so they can stand up, and

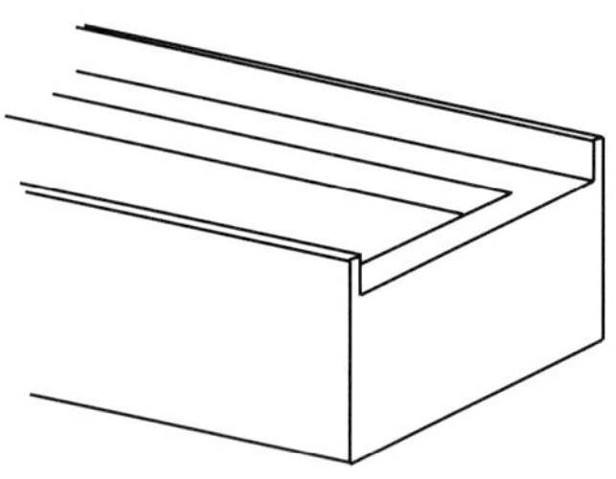

set them loosely into the box. Press the frame down against these supports as far as it will go and proceed with the soldering. When finished, bend the strips as necessary to remove them. Then saw away a section of the wall at one end to make an opening for the lid.

A variation on this trick will be used to hold the second frame into place. Use graphite rod (pencil lead) to maintain an even spacing between the frames. This is where the lid will travel, so the gap between the frames needs to be a specific size. Purchase pencil leads from an office store, or cut away the wood from a standard pencil to uncover the graphite. Rub it on sandpaper as needed to achieve the desired thickness.

Set the graphite pieces into position (they can be held temporarily with a dot of glue if needed), then slide the second frame into place. Apply flux, lay solder chips along the frame and heat until the solder flows. Quench in water and pickle as usual; the graphite will probably fall out by itself. If it gets stuck, pick at it with a scribe to break it out.

Depending on the design of the box, the lid might have a handle or ornamental edge. The sliding action will be smoother if the edges of the lid are slightly rounded and polished.

Screw Closures

To better understand the mechanics of lids that tighten by rotation, step into the "Container Lab," also known as the kitchen. Look at the jars on your shelf and you'll see several variations on the closure shown here. For general use, let's start with the idea that the lid and container are round, or more correctly, segments of cylinders. It's possible to attach a cylindrical mechanism into a square box, for example, but for clarity of illustration we'll work on a cylindrical form.

Bayonet Catch

The bayonet catch can be used on all sorts of boxes and lockets, from large to small and simple to complex. The example shown here uses a basic version; innovative designers will quickly see ways to expand on the idea.

In this example, the container and lid were fabricated from sheet as described elsewhere. A rim was made from 14-gauge wire that fits snugly into the box. It's temporarily set into position inside the box, but not soldered yet. A bezel (an

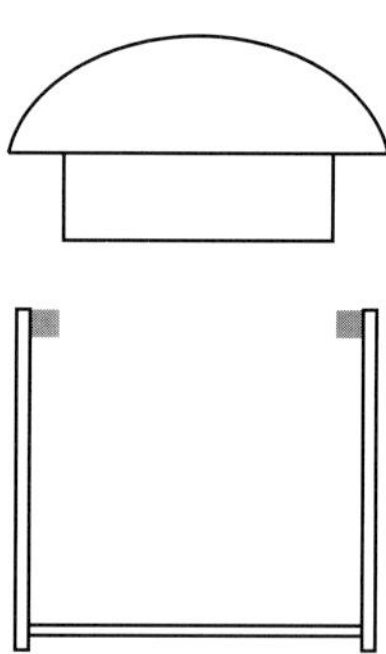

interior wall that fits inside this rim) is soldered onto the lid so that it projects several millimeters into the box.

Small projecting tabs are soldered onto the underside of the lid to engage with the box. These are

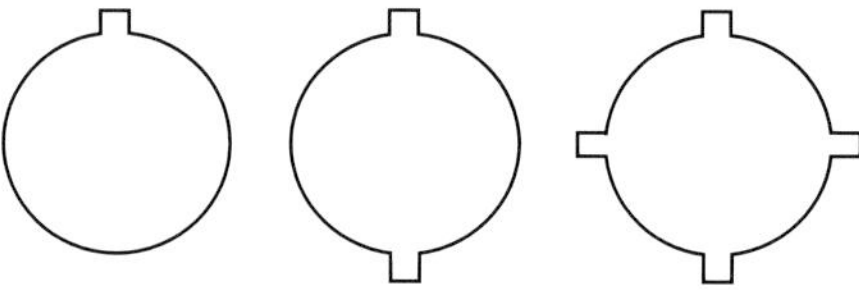

typically small pieces of square wire soldered onto the bezel, but many variations are possible. The catch works with one tab, but two, three or four will also work. If two or more are used, they should be spaced evenly around the lid.

In order for the catch to close tightly, the space between the lid and the top of the tab should be slightly less than the thickness of the rim, in this example, 14-gauge. One way to ensure the correct location of the tab—and location is important—is to saw a slot into the bezel into which the square wire is set. This makes careful checking easy and soldering foolproof.

Set the completed lid onto the box and mark the location of the tabs on the rim. Pull the rim out of the box and cut away a notch from

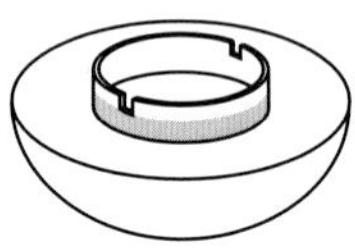

j. e. Paterak, *exist, rub, accept*, locket. Sterling, 18K, pearl, printed paper, 1 1/4"Dia, photos: Robert Diamante. This is from a series titled "Out of Context," a collection of work that uses fragments of printed text. "I love pocketwatches and would like a watchmaker's skill to be present throughout my work."

the outer edge, stopping short of cutting the rim into pieces. With a file, taper the lower edge of the rim slightly outward from each cut. If you work on one side only, the lid will be tightened by rotating in only one direction. If you file a

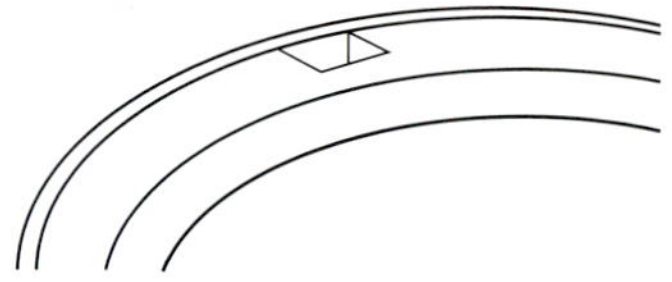

slope on both sides, the lid will tighten by twisting it in either direction.

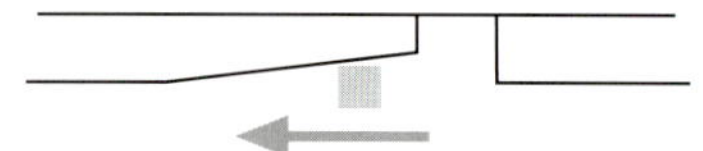

The rim is now soldered into the box, which can be pickled, rinsed and dried. Cut away the small bridge of metal that was holding the rim together—its job is done. File as necessary to allow the tabs to fit. When the lid is rotated, the tab slides along the slope on the lower edge of the rim, pulling the lid on tight.

Making a Full Thread

In the previous example, the interior bezel on the lid made a snug fit into the rim. With a full-thread closure, there needs to be a space be-

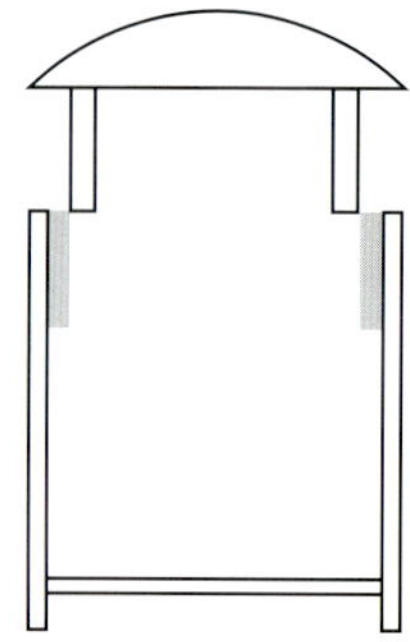

tween the two elements. This is the space where the threads will be. The gap depends on the overall dimensions of the container; in this example, it's about 2 mm. The threads can be attached to the lid, the box, or both.

Think of a thread as a spiral ramp that climbs up the sleeve. It can be made of round, half-round, or square wire; round is easiest to bend but the others are easier to solder. Whatever you choose, wrap the annealed wire around the sleeve tightly, laying each rotation tightly against the preceding one. This will look as if you are wrapping a coil to make giant jump rings.

File the inside of the coil slightly to create a flat facet on the inside edge. This will make a strong joint when soldered onto the sleeve. To create a space between the threads, pull the coil apart. If you do this by holding onto the two ends, it will probably expand evenly. To check the consistency of the gap between threads, slide a piece of sheet—16-gauge in this case—along the coil. "Screw" the coil over the sheet; this will have the effect of making the space between the threads uniform.

Clean the container with Scotch-Brite and screw the coil into position. Apply small pieces of solder about every half inch along the track. Warm the piece uniformly, bringing the torch closer as needed to allow the solder to flow. Quench the piece in water, then pickle and rinse.

A Bayonet Catch

1 Slots are cut in the inner sleeve to hold the wire tabs of this bayonet catch. The space between the lid and the tab (gray in the drawing) must be slightly smaller than the thickness of the rim that was soldered into the box.

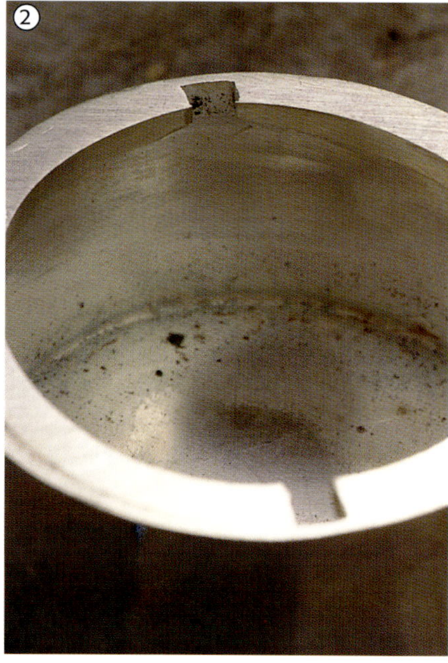

2 File a slope (or ramp) onto the rim, extending outward from the slot. This will create a friction that will lock the lid closed when it's rotated.

A Simple Tab

Test fit the lid into the container. If it doesn't fit (and this is expected, so don't panic), file the thread to reduce its overall diameter. You'll see that this converts the round wire used in the thread into a flat thread that makes a tighter screw mechanism. Things are working out.

All that remains is to solder a tab onto the inside of the box. This

Martha A. Feldhaus,
octagonal box.
Sterling, moonstone,
$3^1/_2$"H x 3"Dia.

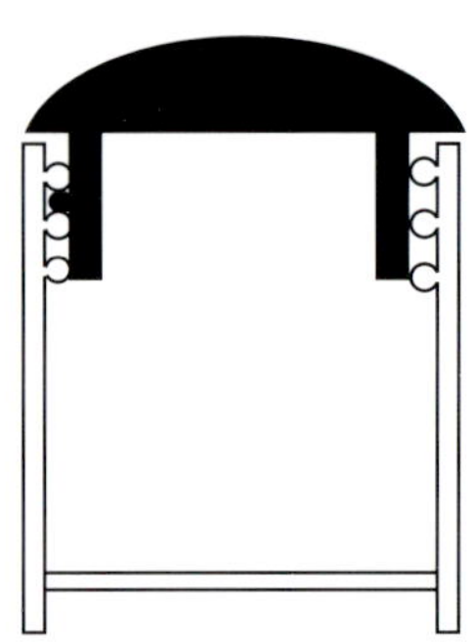

is nothing more than a short finger of metal that will slide along the threaded ramp until the cap is locked into the base. To make a clean and secure joint, drill a hole in the wall of the box, then fit a short length of wire into the hole for soldering. The size of this should match the gap between threads; in this example, it's 16-gauge. The wire is left at a comfortable length for soldering, then trimmed flush on the inside of the lid and cut very short outside. It is rounded slightly with sandpaper.

Test fit the pieces together, paying close attention to any areas of friction. File as needed to allow the top to screw smoothly onto the box.

Making a Double-Threaded Closure

In this slightly more complex threaded closure, both units have a spiraling thread. Instead of a single metal post that travels along the thread, this construction has a full contact thread in both the container and the lid.

As in the first example, the container and lid need to have cylinders that allow space between them for the thread. To create the threads, lay two identical round wires side by side and wrap them in tandem around the sleeve. When you are done, unwind one from the other. Solder one onto the container and the other on the inside of the lid. This is a little easier said than done; expect some filing and fitting to make a proper fit. When soldering, take pains to heat evenly so the coils do not warp.

After the two sections have been quenched, pickled and rinsed, screw them together. If you're lucky, they'll fit at the first attempt. More often, the threads will need some filing to make them slide against one another.

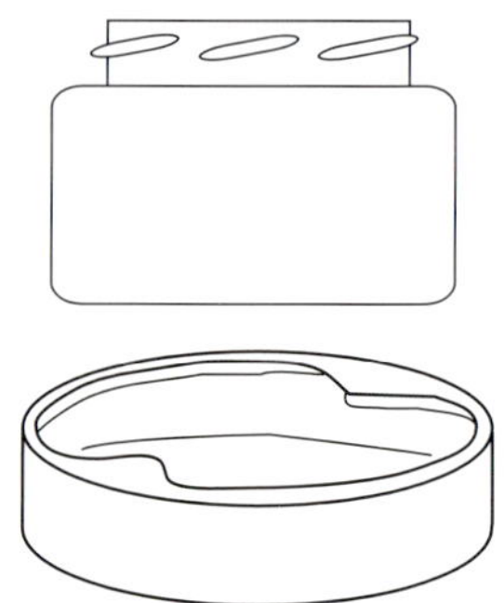

THREADED CLOSURES

1 Screw the coil along a piece of metal to make the opening uniform.

2 File the interior of the coil slightly to create a clean flat surface, then solder it onto the sleeve. To locate a tab accurately, drill a hole and force a bit of wire firmly into it. Trim to size after soldering.

3 Use two wires held side-by-side to make a double coil. Here both sterling and brass are used, but usually the same wire is used for both parts.

Dan Natkiel, pendant. Sterling, glass, plastic, $2\frac{1}{8}$"H x $\frac{5}{8}$"W x $\frac{5}{8}$"D.

Variations

Go back to the kitchen and look at the jars on your shelves. In some cases, you'll see that the threads are three unconnected "ramps" along the sleeve. In others (baby food jars, for instance) you'll find that the catch on the lid is nothing more than a bend in the lip. Think of it this way: the Industrial Epoch has spent millions of dollars refining variations in which containers can be closed by a threaded device. You and I are the beneficiaries of that research.

Jane Campbell, *Box #897,* oval bracelet box. Sterling, 22K, 18K and 14K gold, opals, Chinese writing stones, apatite, mabe pearls, opal, onyx, tourmaline. A six-part box that contains four pieces of jewelry: a pendant on a 21" chain, earrings, and a bracelet. Facing page: the opened box.

3

Catches

Catches can be as simple as a snug fit or as complicated as a hidden mechanical device. In this chapter we'll look at both. While not all boxes and lockets require catches, they usually add sophistication and frequently improve the function of a piece.

Most catches are made toward the end of the construction process, when the location of the hinge has been established. Of course, if the catch will involve soldering, it's assembled before finishing. As a rule, catches are positioned directly opposite the hinge, but there are times when an unexpected off-center catch provides an interesting detail.

General Suggestions

Regardless of the complexity of a catch, it should always be:

- Easy to understand and operate.
- Simple to construct.
- Simple to adjust.
- Capable of removal and repair.

Chris Irick, *Labyrinth*, necklace with pendant. Sterling, copper, watch crystal, steel cable, 2½"D. Layers of pierced and fitted sterling silver are magnified by the lens to increase the illusion of depth. A dark patina on the sterling contributes to the mysterious quality of the piece.

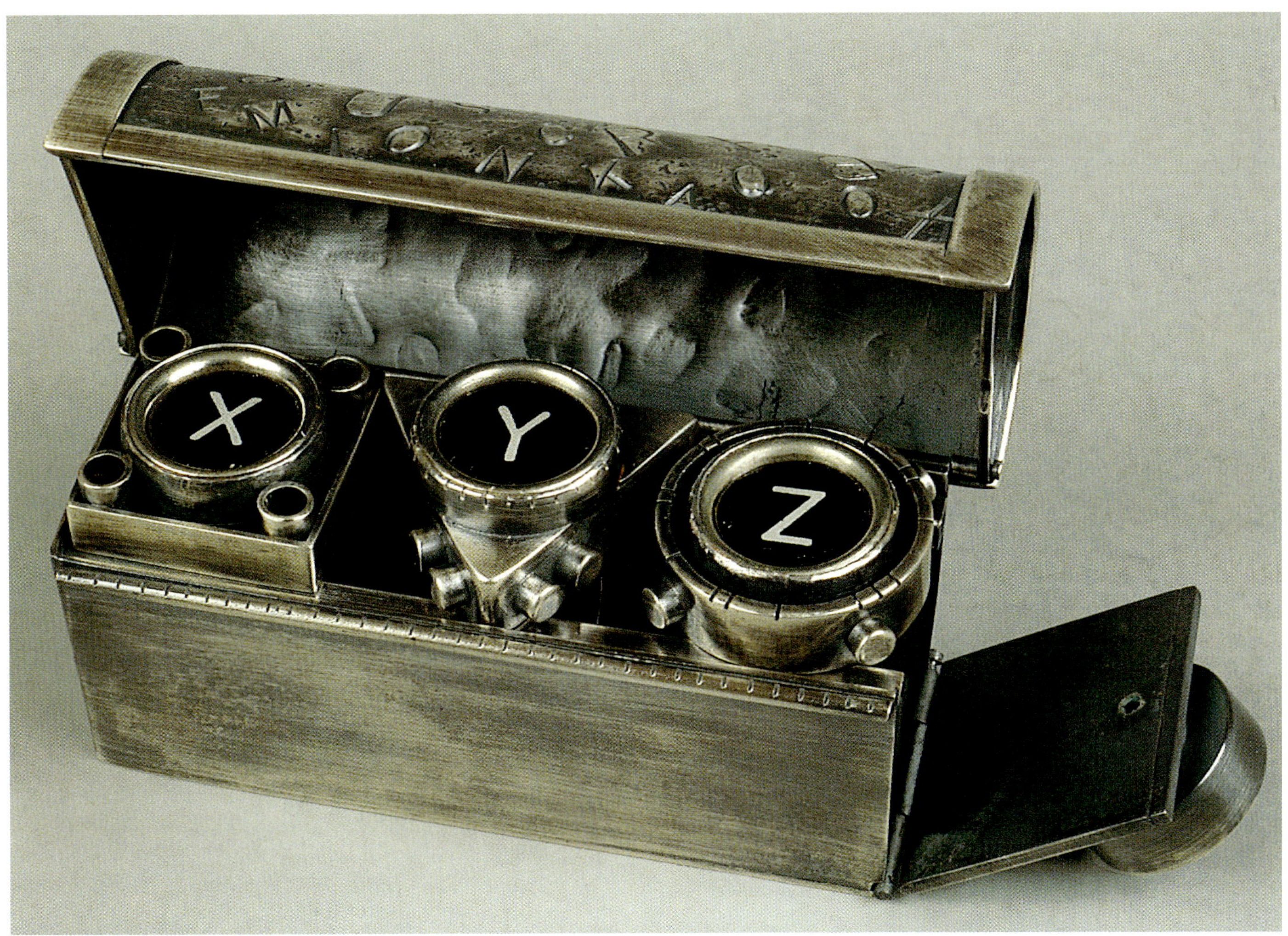

Kiff Slemmons, *Coordinates*. Sterling, typewriter keys, 1 3/8"H x 2 3/8"W x 1 1/2"D, photo: Rod Slemmons. This box opens to allow the side panel, which is also hinged, to open out to the side. The box contains a set of three finger rings.

Bezel Catches

Friction Bezel

Most jewelers think of a bezel as the strip of metal that surrounds and secures a gemstone. The same word is used to describe a rim of relatively thin metal that presses against the inside wall of a box to hold it closed. We see this all the time in containers such as breath mint boxes and film canisters, although we might not use the proper term to describe it.

Bezels can go completely around the box, or they can be partial. Obviously, longer bezels have greater surface area and therefore create greater friction, but partial bezels are usually sufficient for small containers. Bezels can be either in the lid or the bottom unit and are almost always made of the same metal as the box.

It's a common misconception that a tighter fit can be achieved by using a thicker bezel. This is not the case. The friction is achieved as the bezel "leans" against the inside wall of the box (or lid). Thin metal will spring back when opened, retaining its "lean." Thick metal, on the other hand, rubs against the other part and wears down with each use. In addition, thin bezels are easy to readjust when they wear out. If a box loses its grip after a decade or two, you can pull the bezel outward with a burnisher to renew the closure.

Interior Wall as Bezel

This is a variation that solves two problems at once. Any box maker will understand the difficulty of getting an attractive finish on the inside of a metal container. There is no tool that reaches perfectly into the corners! However, there is a way to solve this problem while creating a bezel closure.

The trick is in careful measurement. You can use polished metal, but decorative cardboard, thick paper, or cloth-covered cardboard are useful alternatives. Carefully cut a single panel for the four walls. Make the height of the walls equal to the height of the box plus a millimeter or two. Bend the panel into four walls equal to the perimeter of the box, scoring each bend with a sharp knife to ensure a crisp corner. The walls are pressed into the box, where they should almost snap into place. An interior floor panel of the same material is then pressed in, pushing the walls against the box. The part raised above the box forms a bezel.

Incidentally, this is a classic example of a widely applicable fact of metalworking: proper measurement and construction go a long way toward making elegant objects.

Bobby Hansson, *Trainman's Lunchbox*. Painted tinware.

Dimple Catch

This is one version of an arrangement that appears in boxes and lockets from all around the world. The idea is simple: create two surfaces that slide across one another under tension, then provide some arrangement that makes them want to stay together rather than pull apart. In this example, the bezel has a small raised dot and the interior of the box has a corresponding recess, or dimple. Once the dot slips into the dimple it prefers to stay there; in other words, some pressure is needed to separate the two parts.

In the example shown, the tension is accomplished by making a tight fit between the bezel and the box, and the raised dot is in the bezel. The location of these elements is arbitrary: the raised piece could be on the bezel or in a catch on the outside of a locket. The important thing to understand here is the concept.

To improve the friction of a bezel, add a small dimple in one unit and a matching depression in the other.

The raised dot is made by striking the thin bezel with a bluntly pointed tool like a nail set. (Avoid using anything too sharp so you don't poke right through the metal.) This is done after the bezel is soldered into the lid but before the lid and the box are set together with a hinge pin. The recess is cut with a graver, a drill bit or a rotary bur. The relief in both cases (the dimple and the recess), can be very small.

Hasps

Friction Hasp

With a friction hasp, the friction is not located in the box or locket itself, but is created by a tightness between two pieces that are attached to the outside. In a sense this is a variation on the purse snap described next. Again, there are dozens of configurations for this system. Here's an example to start you thinking.

Attach a bracket to the outside of a box, either by soldering or by means of a cold connection, such as a rivet or miniature bolt. Bend so that the two opposing tips come almost together. Then attach a flat bar of metal to the opposing part of the box or locket, hinged in some way. It can be ornamented or plain, straight or curved, large or delicate. Again, the key here is the concept.

Variations on the friction hasp system are endless ... from simple to complex. It's also possible to combine this system with a padlock or peg.

Brent A. Williams, *Lip Balm Box*. Sterling, moss agate, ½" cube.

Purse Snaps

This is a useful closure that might be familiar from coin purses. When the catch closes, two spheres rub past each other. Because they are attached by a stem that has a little give, the balls push past one another and spring back, making the snap. Several variations are possible, mostly having to do with scale. Try this simple generic version first, then you'll be able to modify the catch to suit your specific needs.

Draw a bead on two pieces of wire, or make *shot* (small metal spheres) by heating pieces of metal as they sit on a soldering block. This can be done in any of the jewelry metals, but silver and gold yield a better result than copper or brass.

If the shot cools too rapidly, the surface wrinkles like a raisin. This texture is usually unattractive and will detract from the smooth operation of the catch. To minimize the wrinkling, heat the metal until it draws naturally into the sphere, then slowly withdraw the heat, lifting the torch away as if in slow motion. This allows the sphere to cool uniformly and makes it more likely to harden into a smooth ball. If it doesn't work the first time, reflux the metal and try again.

Even at its best, this process will create an oval lump. The shape can be refined with files, a process made simpler by gripping the wire in a pin vise. It's also possible to secure the wire in a flexible shaft machine to mimic a lathe and refine its shape by rotating it against sandpaper.

Here's an easy way to make a sphere uniform: chuck the wire into a flex shaft and run it against sandpaper in decreasing grits until you have the finish you need.

Solder the two "lollipops" onto the edges of the box lid. The joints need to be strong: remember to clean and contour both sides so the pieces make a precise fit. The location of the attachments is somewhat arbitrary; the working of the catch will be created by bending the stems after they are attached.

When the pieces have been pickled, rinsed and dried, temporarily assemble the hinge and close the box. Polish the spheres to allow them to slip smoothly against each other. Bend the two stems so the balls connect well enough to have tension, but not so much that they are hard to pull apart. Though difficult to describe in words, the adjustment will be obvious when you have the catch in your hands.

A Pinching Hasp

In this catch, a U-shaped hasp will hold the box closed by wrapping around the flange on both pieces. A rivet through the hasp will keep it attached to the lower half of the

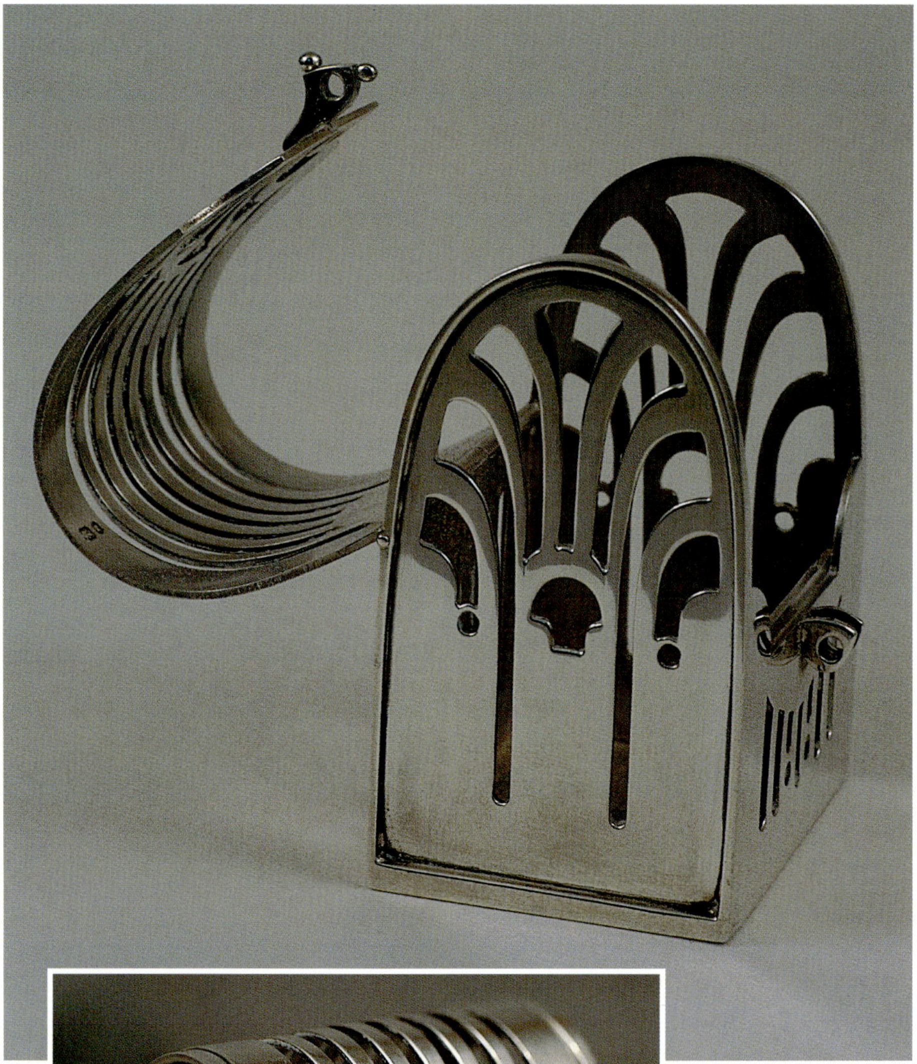

Paula Wolfe, *Pomander*. Sterling, 2½"H x 2"W x 1½"D.

This hasp rotates outward from the single rivet. In its open position, the lid is free to lift. If the catch loosens with use, it is easy to squeeze the legs closer together to renew the friction.

box while allowing it to pivot outward for opening. To make the hasp, bend a rectangle of sheet over two pieces of sheet the same gauge as the flange. The goal is to create a U with parallel sides (shaded area).

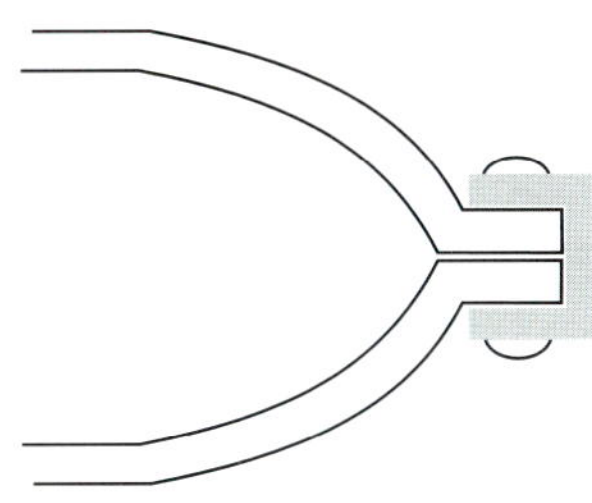

Drill a small hole through the hasp, taking care to keep the drill bit vertical. Slide the hasp onto the double-layers of flange with the box closed and drill through the flange using the holes in the hasp as a guide. Remove the hasp and saw out from the lid a small triangle from the flange that has the hole in its center.

Premelt a tiny bit of solder on the underside of this triangle and solder it onto the flange of the lower unit. Push a steel wire or piece of pencil lead (i.e., graphite rod) through the holes to keep the pieces in alignment. Clean the pieces after soldering and test the assembly with temporary pins through the hinge and catch. It might be necessary to trim away a little of the curved part of the U to allow the hasp to open fully. When you're sure the mechanism works, dismantle the pieces so they can be patinated, polished and in every other way taken to their final finish. Reassemble and lock the pin in both the hinge and the clasp with light riveting.

Spring Catches

Push-Release Catch

In the very large category of spring catches, the push-release catch is probably the most broadly used. Variations on this arrangement account for scores of catches used on boxes, compacts, watchcases, lockets and pill boxes. The sense of the mechanism is illustrated in the drawing: the catch includes a trigger, a hook and a snag. The hook grabs onto the snag to keep the box closed. When the trigger is pressed the hook slides back, releases the snag and allows the box to open. The hook is springy enough to return to its original location, so the box will snap closed when the lid falls.

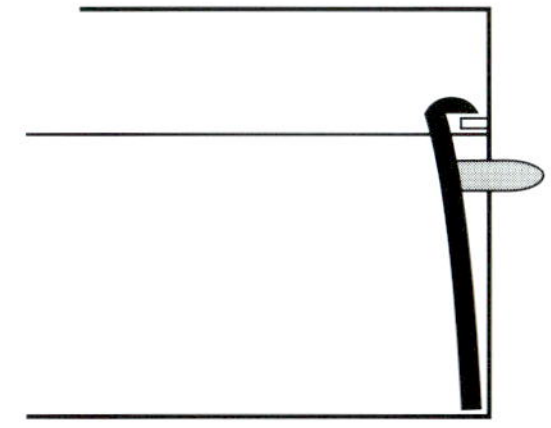

In the end, the catch requires that all the parts work together, so it really doesn't matter which comes first. In this example, you might start by making the hook. For a small box like the one shown below, I've used a flattened piece of 16-gauge wire. Score a V-groove near one end, bend it to a right an-

This is a familiar catch with many possible variations. Pressing the trigger pushes the spring-loaded catch backward, releasing its grip on a small horizontal shelf attached to the inside of the lid.

gle, and reinforce the score with solder. The top is then filed to create a crisp 90° angle and a rounded top. The top is the surface the snag will rub against as the box is closed, so it must be curved to allow it to fall back under pressure. For an example, look at the latch of a door in your house and compare that shape to a deadbolt. The latch is curved so it will retract as the door is pressed closed.

Adding a Trigger

Next, attach a trigger. This can be as simple as another piece of round wire, or as fancy as a bezel-set stone or a cast ornament. If it is small enough to fit through a hole in the wall of the box (as in this example), the trigger can be finished at this stage. If it's larger, you will need to devise a way to attach the larger "cover" piece after the stem is passed through the wall.

The snag is typically a small horizontal shelf soldered into the lid, but it can be as simple as a line cut with a graver or a separating disk. The scale of the box will suggest the best solution. When all the parts are made and have been test-fitted into position (and after the box is complete and taken to its final finish), the hook unit is slid into place and attached with a cold connection that will not remove its temper. This can be a pair of rivets, a bracket attached inside the box, screws or tabs. Once assembled, the catch is fine-tuned by filing and sanding to allow a small pressure on the trigger to release the hook.

Internal Tension Spring

This appealing closure has many applications, but is perhaps best recognized from its use in the cigarette lighter and its ancestor, a pocket-sized container called a matchsafe. The catch is hidden and rugged, and allows the box to snap open with the flick of a thumb.

The secret of the catch is a cam or lug (a built-up section) on the middle knuckle of the hinge. This is under tension from a bar of springy metal, as shown in the diagram. I think of it this way: where does the spring *want* to be? In this box, the answer is vertical; the bar of springy nickel silver used here wants to stand vertical and will push against anything that gets in its way as it tries to do so. Because of the location of the cam on the center knuckle of the hinge, this pressure pushes the lid open or holds it closed.

Matchsafe commercially produced in Great Britain, circa 1910.

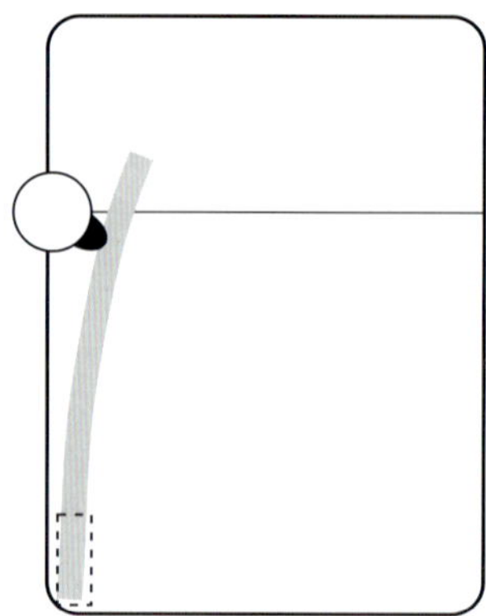

Picture the rotation of the lid through its full arc from closed to open. First you'll notice that the cam is always in contact with the hinge. This tension makes the action feel solid and sturdy. As the cam presses against the spring, the tension increases, reaching its maximum at the point where the cam is at right angles to the spring.

Joe Muench, *Beggar's Box*. Brass, steel, 6"H x 6"W x 6"D, photos: David Kingsbury. This dramatic box is constructed entirely from found objects, including the water meter cover from the artist's house. The piece was assembled in such a way that the ferrous and non-ferrous metals could be separated—the first thing a scrap metal dealer does.

In order to make the hinge work smoothly, the location of this spot is critical. You'll note that in this

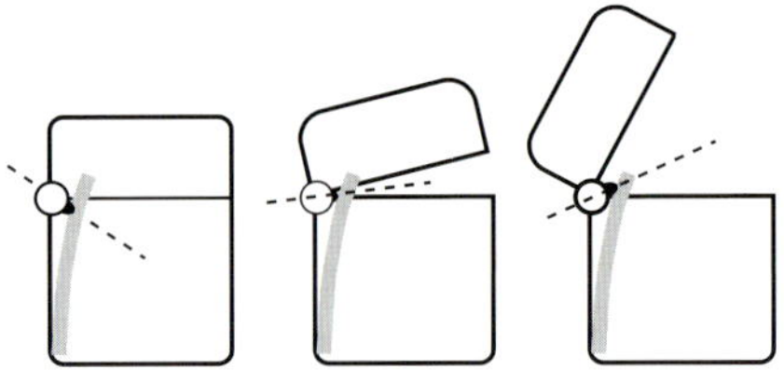

example, the maximum tension falls when the lid is halfway between open and closed; let's call this the midposition.

In a properly built tension spring, the lid will stay "poised" in the midposition. A small movement toward closing will alter the angles enough that the lid will snap shut. A small movement toward opening will cause the spring to press against the other side of the cam and throw the lid open.

The degree of tension depends on the thickness, material and condition of the spring. It can be made of steel or work-hardened brass, nickel silver or sterling. To preserve its hardness, this strip must be attached into the box without the use of heat. One solution is to solder a length of tubing into the bottom of the box. The spring is then forced into this tubing, where friction holds it in place.

In the photo to the right, the tubing has been flattened to form an oval cross section. The spring, in this case a piece of thick nickel silver wire pounded flat, has been tapered and sharpened so it will drive into the sleeve like a nail going into a wall. Keep in mind that the nickel is much harder than the sterling tubing, so it will cut its own path as it's tapped into place. Like a nail, if this is driven and pulled out several times, the tight fit will be lost, but if driven in only once it will hold very well.

Another solution would be to rivet the spring down low in the box, either through the bottom or the lower side. It's also possible to bend the spring so it makes a snug fit simply by being pressed into place. This requires careful fitting,

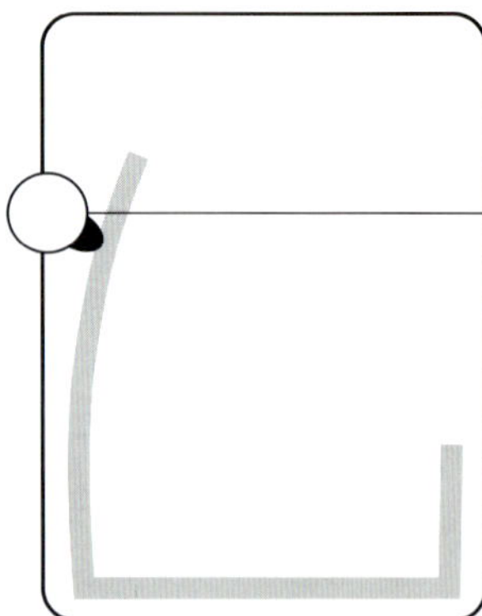

but it's an elegant solution and worth trying.

The thick cam on the center knuckle rubs against the leaf spring, keeping the lid closed or open, depending on the angle of the lid.

Making the Hinge

Knuckles for a hinge like the one just described should be made of thick tubing to allow for years of wear. Note that other applications of this spring hinge involve less stress and can therefore be made of conventional tube knuckles.

One way to secure a spring into a box is to solder a section of tubing like this. The spring is filed to a point and driven into place like a nail. Barbs (like those on a fishhook) can even be added to increase the grip.

Jason Morrissey, pocket locket. Sterling, citrine, $1\frac{1}{4}$"H x $1\frac{1}{2}$"Dia, photos: Robert Diamante. The double action lends a drama to the act of opening this palm-sized container, bringing the user into the intimacy of the piece.

Mariko Kusumoto, *Father's Room*, music box with movement. Brass, nickel silver, stones, wax, found objects, 9"H x 10½"W x 2¾"D, photo: Hap Sakwa. "My father is a Buddhist priest, and I grew up in a temple which was founded 400 years ago. As time goes by, my memories become stronger and more vivid. This feeling is the inspiration of my artwork today."

Make a three-knuckle hinge in the usual way: prepare the seat, solder a single knuckle into the center of one trough, mark its location on the other side and solder the two outer tubes into position. Check the hinge to be certain it has no gaps and works properly. Pat yourself on the back.

If this is your first time making this hinge, it might be prudent to go through a dry run. Placement of the lug is very important! Set a piece of brass or copper into place to mimic the spring. Remember, it should stand straight up, vertical. When you assemble the hinge (put the top on and slide a temporary pin through the hinge), the copper should be rubbing against the center tube.

Open the box slowly to the mid-position and make a scribe mark on the tube exactly where it's in contact with the mock spring. This is the proper location for the cam. Disassemble the hinge and file a flat facet on the center knuckle at the marked point. This facet will show the location clearly. Confirm that any surface contaminant has been scraped away and ensure that the pieces about to be soldered will make a good fit.

Cut a piece of stout square wire (e.g., 10-gauge) or a similar block from thick sheet. Premelt solder onto the base of this, then set it onto the fluxed facet on the tube.

Left: Kristina Kada, *A Core of Gold*, locket. Fine silver, 18K, 1"Dia, photo: Ralph Gabriner. The outer shell was cast as a single hollow sphere, then cut open. Disks of gold were dapped and soldered to platforms that were then assembled into the shells. A basic hinge and friction clasp add to the refined elegance.

Solder into place, pickle and rinse. The cam should be rounded and smooth so it rolls easily along the spring. Use a combination of files, sandpaper and polishing wheels to accomplish this.

Assembling a conventional hinge is usually the easiest part of the process: just set the lid into place and slide a hinge pin through the aligned knuckles. Not so in the case of spring hinges. All spring hinges, including this one, are under tension all the time. When you try to set the lid into place, the spring will be in the way—that's its job. Press the tubing against the spring as you lower the lid into place.

Depending on the amount of tension you've created, this can be an awkward chore. It's often handy to have a friend standing by to slide the hinge pin into place. The process will go much more easily if the pin is tapered. When working alone, try this: taper a length of wire that will be the hinge pin and clamp it in a vise so most of the wire sticks out. You can then force the lid into place and press the box along the wire to set the pin. Test the action, make adjustments if necessary, and lightly rivet the ends of the pin to secure it into place.

Kathleen Browne, *A Gambler's Fate*. Sterling, resin, plastics, 5"H x 2½"W x 1"D.

Kee-Ho Yuen, box. Sterling, Corian®, gold plating, 4"H x 5"W x 4$\frac{1}{4}$"Dia.

Hidden and Trick Catches

Larger books than this one could be written just about trick catches. This is only a brief sampling of the field, but for the cagey craftsman, it might be enough to whet the appetite. The examples described below can be used exactly as shown, but more likely you'll invent variations that make each catch uniquely diabolical.

Gravity Trigger

This catch is illustrated in a box with a sliding lid, but variations can be developed for other styles of closures. In this case, when the lid is closed, it appears to lock without any apparent action. No buttons are pushed, but the catch is simple to release when you know the secret.

The holding device is simply a piece of sheet metal attached to the inside of the box with a single rivet. The rivet must be loose enough to allow the metal to rotate freely.

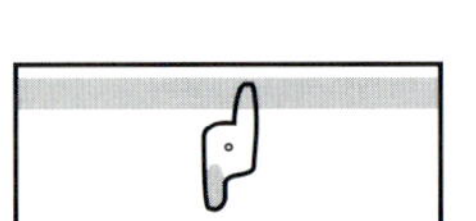

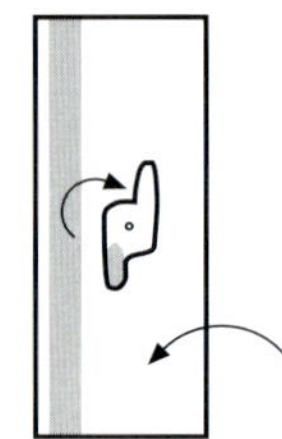

When the box is right-side up, the weight on the lower end of the catch pivots the bar upright where the tip slides into a slot in the lid.

To open the box, turn it on its side. The catch rotates 90°, allowing the lid to be slid open. As simple as gravity!

Patty Bolz,
neckpiece/enhancer.
22K yellow gold,
14K white gold back,
aquamarine, diamonds,
1¾"H, photos:
Robert Diamante.

Hook Style

This is typically a variation on the push-release catch described earlier in this chapter. The difference is that instead of having a trigger plainly visible on the outside of the box, this catch uses a cam inside the box to push the hook free of the snag. Again the permutations are endless, but here's one way it can be used.

The photo below shows the inside of the front panel of a box. The spring has been cut from sheet metal, forged to make it springy, and riveted into place at the bottom. When the lid comes down, a platform catches on the hook and the box is sealed shut. From the outside, there appears to be no way to release the catch. Instead what we see on the outside is an ornamental medallion.

Right: Glenda Rowley, potpourri container. Sterling, nickel silver, brass, copper, rubber, 2"H x 2"Dia.

MAKING A LEAF-STYLE TRICK CATCH

1 This trick catch is operated by rotating a device on the outside. When the cam pushes the spring sideways, the catch is released.

2 Note that a square rivet is used to lock the two disks for proper rotation.

3 This is the outside of the same box. The mechanism is built into an ornamental disk. By using several of these catches, it's possible to make a sort of combination lock.

Caryn L. Hetherston, *The Duality Between Action and Prayer*, box. Sterling, 22K, 14K, rutilated amethyst, fine silver chain, 4¼"H x 2"W x 4"D, photos: Peter Groesbeck.

The medallion is free to rotate on an axle. This moves a cam against the hook, pressing it sideways to release the lid. It's possible to relate the ornamentation of the medallion to the correct position for opening.

Leaf Style

This is a variation on the catch just described. A thin piece of springy metal is attached to the underside of the lid in such a way that when the box is closed the spring drops down to snag on the inside of the box. Anyone who has gotten a box of plastic wrap stuck in a kitchen drawer knows how effective this can be.

Nancy Deal, locket.
Bronze, sterling, nickel, steel, glass lens, $2^{1}/_{4}$"Dia.

Chris Irick, *Contained*, locket. Sterling, copper, brass, hydrostone, 4"H x 2½"W x 1"D. This locket is worn in the manner of a watch chain. The outer shell was die-formed and constructed, using banding and rivets to create a mechanical motif. The inside was filled with hydrostone (a commercial casting material) and a niche was carved to hold the wrapped element.

To release the spring, a disk is mounted inside the box in a way that will allow it to be rotated from outside. This can be an obvious handle or a detail hidden in the ornamentation. The disk is either cut with a cam or mounted eccentrically (its rotating hole off center) so that when turned it presses upward against the spring.

Integrated Spring

This ingenious catch was devised by Mary Schimpff Webb for her *Armadillo Box* (shown on pages 116–117). The body of the animal is an oval box that opens on a hinge located just above its tail. The box snaps closed when a platform on the inside of the lid is engaged by a spring-loaded hook. To open the box, we press on the armadillo's nose. A wire here runs through the head and pushes the hook away from the platform.

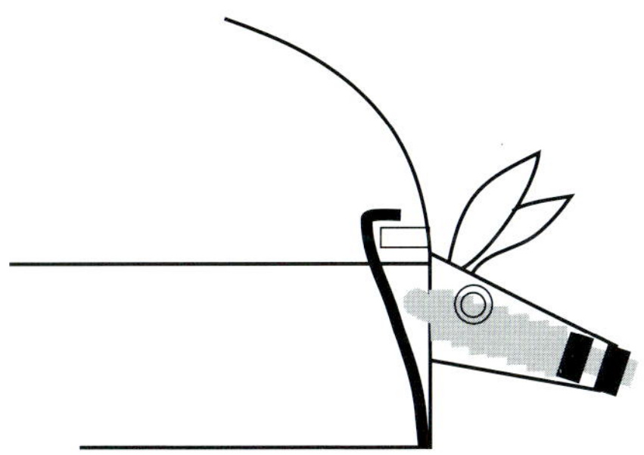

To allow the nose-trigger to spring back into position, the rod running through the head is encased in a coil spring, this one scavenged from a pen. A ring was soldered onto the rod to engage the spring. The rod with the spring in place was then inserted into the head through the nose (ugh!). A sterling ring was soft soldered onto the tip of the nose to make it impossible for the trigger mechanism to come out the way it went in.

This page and facing page:
Mary Schimpff Webb, *Armadillo Box*.
Sterling, 3"H x 4"W x $2\frac{1}{2}$"D,
photos: Robert Diamante.

Basics & Practices

The various steps in making boxes and lockets often involve basic procedures such as measuring, soldering and finishing. Whether closing a corner or attaching a knuckle, a torch is essential to the process. At first, it's enough to know how to light the torch, but as your work becomes more complex and you grow more comfortable handling the tool, it's important to deepen your understanding. This is true not only of the torch, but of many other tools and procedures.

This chapter is, therefore, a kind of information warehouse—advice and options that relate to many of the techniques described throughout the rest of the book. Soldering, for example, is used in almost every process described in the preceding pages, so here you'll find information about soldering tools and tricks. Because tubing is so important, this chapter will tell you how to make it, cut it and size it. And then there's ... well, you get the idea. If we hadn't thought of a catchy heading like "Basics and Practices," we would have called this chapter "Miscellaneous."

Teri Blond, *Cowboy Box.* Painted tinware, photo: Bobby Hansson.

Brent A. Williams, box. Brass, $^{5}/_{8}$"H x $1^{5}/_{8}$"Dia.

Soldering Methods

The most common and obvious way to solder is to set the fluxed components together, lay a small piece of solder across the joint, and heat it up. As a rule of thumb, simpler is better, so this should generally be your first choice. But sometimes more is needed.

When pieces will not stay together by themselves, it may be necessary to tie them together with wire. The best material for this is an annealed blackened steel wire called *binding wire,* available from jewelry supply companies. Galvanized steel wire from a hardware store can also be used, as can nickel silver wire, but these are harder to bend around the pieces.

Joining irregular shapes may require a little more forethought. First, figure out the lines of tension that are needed—where exactly you need to press, and at what angle—then provide a handle for that line. In some cases, this means adding a piece of wire with loops, or cutting notches into an edge that will be cut away later.

Wrap the binding wire loosely into place and twist the ends together. Then grip it with flat-nose pliers and give a twist, creating a Z-bend. Repeat these steps as needed to cinch the binding wire, pulling the pieces into position for soldering. The bends allow the wire to stretch as the work expands with heat.

When using ferrous binding wire, remember to quench the wire in water and remove it before pickling; otherwise, the object will become copper-plated. Some suppliers sell a stainless steel binding wire that can go directly into the pickle.

Clamps

These are reusable, steel wire devices that work like binding wire to hold pieces in position for soldering. As with wire, they should be used sparingly because they rob heat from the joint. It's better to spend a little time creating the right clamp for the job than to overload a piece with several ill-fitting braces.

I make spring clamps from recycled bits of steel wire that start their life as coat hangers, paper clips and hair pins. These are usually made of tough tool steel that will stand up to repeated heatings. The simplest version of a clamp is a simple bent wire. This can be made stiffer by hammering on the bend, changing the cross section from round to flat. The tips are usually flattened slightly, but they can be given other shapes.

Clamps can be made from various steel wires, including paper clips and coat hangers. These are used during soldering and gluing.

Self-Locking Clamp

A variation of the spring clamp is the self-locking (or cross-lock) clamp. This can be easily tailored to meet specific needs. Start by wrapping the wire around a rod several times to create a coil spring. Shape one leg to the desired form and bend the other leg so it leaves the coil about one-quarter of the way around. (If the coil were a clock with the first leg at twelve o'clock, the other leg should point to three o'clock.)

Bend a sharp angle in this wire no closer than a half inch to the coil. Put in a second bend to bring the legs parallel, then push the second leg past the first. This will create a pinching action at rest. Some minor adjustments will be necessary to bring the legs into contact. To use, squeeze the legs near the coil to open the clamp and set it into place. When released, it will grip the pieces.

With a little practice, these clamps become very simple to make and can be made or modified as dictated by each situation.

Soldering Investment

Using binding wire can be awkward when working with multiple small pieces such as the knuckles of a hinge. For these cases you might prefer soldering investment, a plaster-like white powder with special ingredients that allow it to cure quickly and withstand high temperatures.

First, assemble the pieces to be soldered and secure them with a tiny drop of adhesive such as epoxy or cyanoacrylate ("Super Glue"). Alternatively, the pieces can be pressed into clay or wax.

Mix up a small quantity of powder and water according to the directions on the package. Spoon the yogurty mix over the assembled pieces, being careful to leave sections of each joint exposed for soldering. If necessary, scrape the drying investment away to expose a joint. Allow the investment to dry as described on the package—typically around 15 minutes. Set the work under a light or on a radiator, or use a hair dryer to hasten the drying.

Warm the piece with a gentle flame to burn off the glue (don't inhale the fumes); then add flux and pieces of solder. Heat in the usual way until the solder flows. Check to ensure that each joint is complete, then quench the piece in water. The investment will crumble into powder. Use a toothbrush to remove any tiny grains that remain.

Soldering: The Givens

There are as many ways to solder as there are metalsmiths. In the end, of course, there are only two results: success, or the opportunity to try again.

Many aspects of soldering are constant, determined by metallurgy and physics. *Brazing* (the correct term for what is also called "silver soldering" or "hard soldering") can only take place at temperatures that approach the melting point of the metals being joined. No matter how you do it, that's a given.

Soldering investment is dripped and molded around small parts to hold them in place. The investment is allowed to dry, then soldering continues as usual. The investment will fall away when the piece is quenched.

Above: Kathy Hart, *Tzedakah (Charity) Box.* Sterling, fine silver, plique-à-jour enamel, garnet cabachon knob, 4½"H x 3"W x 2"D, photo: L. Stein.

Above right: Addison Saunders, *Maine Tourmaline Box.* 18K, 22K, tourmaline. The top of this elegant box is a natural-shaped cross-section of a bi-color tourmaline gem that weighs 152.5 carats.

Right: Lorraine Lenskold, *Icon Pillbox.* Sterling, 14K, carved and dyed bone, 1"H x 1"W x ½"D, photo: Ralph Gabriner.

Another given is the need to minimize oxidation on the surface. This is not a problem with pure metals such as fine silver or fine gold, which form no significant oxides. When using alloys like sterling, or base metals like copper or brass, however, the need to prevent oxidation becomes more critical.

One way to achieve this is to solder in an oxygen-free environment. Besides doing your work in high-earth orbit, this can be done in sealed chambers or with special torches that allow inert gas to flow over the soldering area and push oxygen away. These torches generally use an electric arc instead of a flame and are most commonly used for aluminum, steel and exotic ferrous alloys. They are called tungsten inert gas (TIG) or magnesium inert gas (MIG) welders.

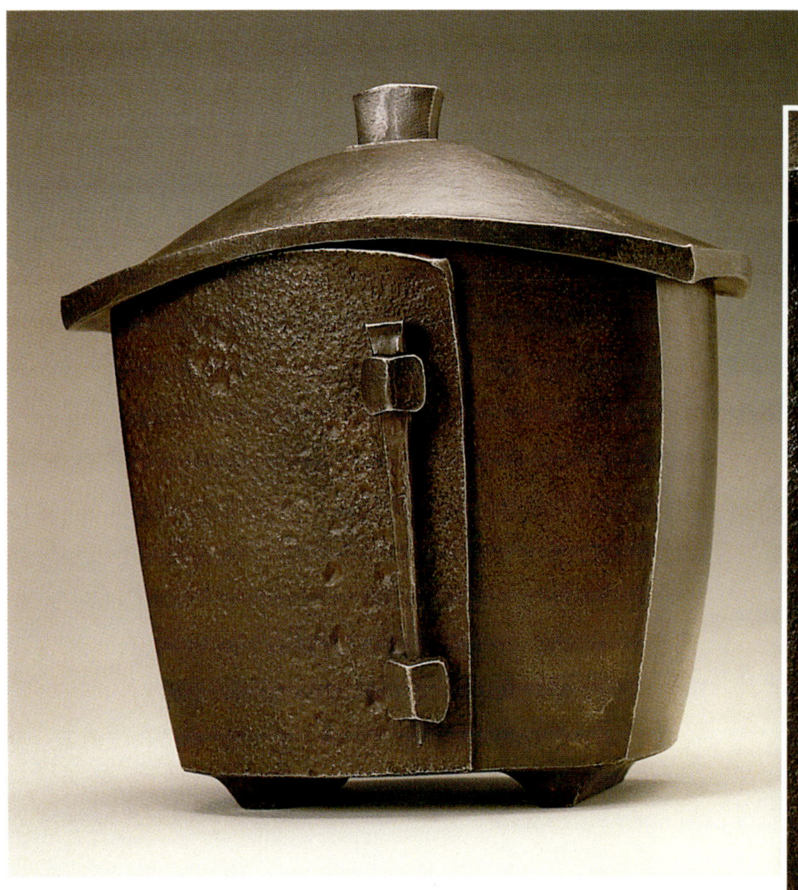

Stephen Yusko, *Nail Box.* Steel, $8\frac{1}{2}$"H x 8"W x 5"D, photos: Robert O'Neil. The body of the box is made of five formed steel panels. The joints are welded, ground down, sanded and textured. The bottom of the box is made of a steel panel with the feet sunken in and then raised to produce crisp, faceted lines. The handle and nail are riveted in place, then the box is patinated with ferric nitrate and sealed with wax.

Torches

Most metalsmiths working in gold, silver and copper alloys use torches for soldering. These torches come in a wide range of models, are relatively cheap to buy and operate, and provide great flexibility. The choice of which torch is right for you depends on your price range, the type of work you do and personal taste. All the torches described here can be used for most of the tasks that come up in a metalsmith's studio, but they are suited to different projects. A person whose most frequent task is attaching wires to gold earrings would choose a smaller torch than someone who principally makes large brass belt buckles.

The three most common fuel gases used in metalsmithing studios are acetylene, propane and butane, the first being the most common. A fourth fuel, natural gas (or "city gas"), is often used in schools and commercial shops, but for home studios, it's rarely worth the cost of the professionally installed plumbing required. Torches made to run on natural gas will work with propane.

These gases can be purchased locally through welding supply

companies. Ask for all relevant safety information and turn to the supplier first if you have a question or suspect a problem. Small tanks are usually bought outright, while larger tanks may be either purchased or leased. Propane tanks are sometimes filled while you wait; acetylene tanks are always swapped. You don't own a particular acetylene tank for good; instead you buy an initial tank and then trade in empty ones for new, refilled tanks.

Tanks are pumped full of gas under high pressure, like a balloon blown up to maximum capacity. Especially when full, the gas will come hissing out with extreme force—far too fast to stay lit. For this reason, each tank is fitted with a regulator, a pressure control valve that will harness or regulate the flow of the gas as it comes out.

David Jones, *I'm Curly,* box. Sterling, 18K, copper, 19th-century glass button, 1950s Three Stooges Flicker, 6"H x 1½"W x 1½"D, photo: Walker Montgomery.

Regulators

Regulators are specific to each gas: each type of regulator has unique threads so it cannot accidentally be screwed onto the wrong tank. Rules for regulators are as simple as they are important.

Rules for Regulators

- Never force the threads.
- Never use grease, wax, tape or oil on the threads.
- Always check for leaks around the threads after changing tanks.
- Never try to fix or adapt a regulator yourself.

To check for leaks, screw the regulator onto its tank and tighten firmly with a wrench. Open the knob on the tank and brush soapy water over the threaded coupling. A leak will be indicated by a cluster of small bubbles. Tighten the nut further; if the bubbling doesn't stop, close the tank, remove the regulator and take both outdoors. Call your welding shop and ask for advice; they might come to pick it up. The problem could be the result of damaged threads on the tank or in the regulator, or a piece of grit in the coupling.

It's common and relatively inexpensive to repair regulators; any welding supply company can have it done by a qualified technician. If the problem is in the tank itself, you can expect a replacement cylinder at no charge.

Sources of Oxygen

The most significant difference among torches is not their fuel but their source of oxygen, the element needed to support combustion. Some torches draw the oxygen they need from the atmosphere. You can recognize these because they have one knob. Other torches use pure oxygen that comes in a tank. Torches that use bottled oxygen have two knobs, one for fuel and one for oxygen.

The atmosphere around us contains roughly 20 percent oxygen. Most of the rest is nitrogen and traces of carbon dioxide, neither of which has much to do with burning. Thus, a given volume of atmosphere contains only one-fifth the oxygen of the same volume coming directly from a tank. This explains why torches that burn pure oxygen are so much hotter than atmosphere-fuel torches. Note that size and heat are not related: a flame fed by pure oxygen may be very small and still be much hotter than a large atmosphere flame.

Flame Types

Since every torch flame is a combination of fuel and oxygen, it makes sense that the proportions of the two can be adjusted. When every molecule of fuel gas combines with its maximum load of oxygen molecules so there is nothing left over, the result is called a *neutral flame* (number 2 in the drawing). If there is more than enough fuel, the flame is called *reducing* (1); excess oxygen makes an *oxidizing flame* (3).

In atmosphere-fuel torches, the mix is preset by the manufacturer, determined by air intake holes somewhere in the torch. These let in just enough air to balance the stream of fuel. If more fuel is allowed to pass through the torch, more air is automatically drawn in to maintain the balance.

In oxygen-fed torches the mix is manual. Start by lighting the fuel gas. Oxygen by itself won't burn, so if you try to light the wrong gas, nothing will happen. When the

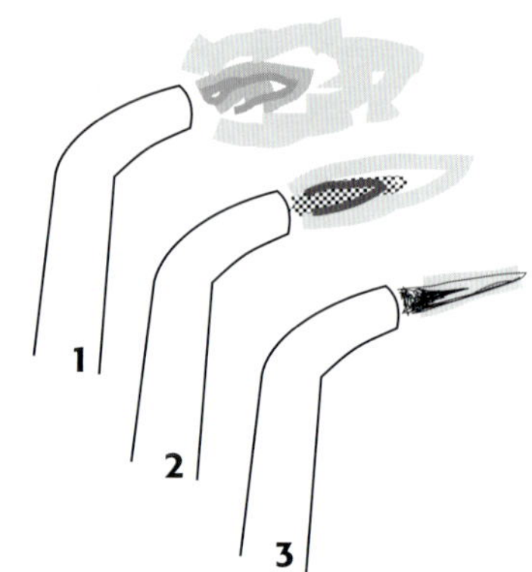

flame is lit, slowly add oxygen: the yellow fuel-only flame will turn blue and narrow. Continue slowly adding oxygen until the flame divides itself into a pale blue inner

Above: Micki Lippe, *Birthday Box.* Sterling, 22K, 2½" cube, photo: Richard Nicol. This box was made as a present from the artist to her husband. Each gold bar represents a year of his life; the other forms represent children and events in their lives. From the accompanying poem: "The box is not perfectly square; The bottom does not sit level; Life is not perfect, nor does it often sit level. The small square hole in the top; For memories, put them in…."

Left: Jon Michael Route, box. Pewter, brass, 4"H x 4"W x 5"D.

cone and a dark blue outer cone. This is a neutral flame and the one you'll use most of the time.

Add more fuel and the flame will get larger and more "bushy." It may also show intermittent flashes of yellow. This is a reducing flame: it reduces the risk of oxidation and is sometimes called a "clean flame." Use it when annealing, depletion gilding, and melting sterling or karat gold.

You can create a neutral flame by turning down the fuel and then adding more oxygen; but be careful not to add too much oxygen, or you will create an oxidizing flame. The torch will make a high-pitched, hissing noise and the flame will become paler and more pointy. There is no reason to use an oxidizing flame in metalworking.

Ken Cory, *Tape Measure.* Sterling, garnet, bone, steel, 2"H x 2"W x 3/4"D, photo: Lynn Thompson. Yes, the tape measure really works. Cory was well-known for adding whimsy and elegance to familiar objects and preoccupations.

Tubing

Anyone who makes boxes will sooner or later need to use tubes, so it's important to understand how they're made and used. In addition to length, tubing size is described by its inside diameter (i.d.), outside diameter (o.d.) and wall thickness.

Tubes can be made in the studio or purchased, usually in foot-long sections. Commercial tubing is made through a continuous casting process and therefore has no seams. It's usually sold in a hard or half-hard condition. Some suppliers offer a range of tube diameters and several wall thicknesses, but most have a relatively limited selection.

If you have a drawplate, you can reduce the diameter of tubing—a process that will automatically increase the wall thickness at the same time. To do this, take a piece of brass or sterling wire about an inch long that fits snugly into the tube. Slide the wire about

Albion Smith, container. Sterling, reticulation silver, tourmaline, citrine, quartz, 3 5/8"H x 3"W x 3"D, photo: Carol Holaday.

Above: Frances J. Pickens, box. Sterling, copper, scarabs.

Left: Micki Lippe, *Spirit House Neckpiece.* Sterling, 22K, red jasper, 3"H, photo: Richard Nicol. "I became aware of the importance of a safe place, a refuge from the hectic and sometimes threatening world we live in. A 'spirit house' is a place of safe-keeping for your soul, your spirit. I am attempting on a very personal level to relate to the difficulties and triumphs we all have in our lives."

1/4" into the tube and solder it there, taking a moment to anneal the tube while you're at it.

Quench, rinse and dry the piece; then file the wire to a gradual taper that blends smoothly into the tube. Pull this through a drawplate exactly as you would draw wire, moving sequentially through smaller and smaller holes. It's especially important that the pulling motion is exactly perpendicular to the drawplate. If you pull at an angle, the tube will become curved. To correct this, pull the tube through the same hole while angling the motion opposite the curve. As with wire drawing, it might be necessary to anneal the metal or re-file the tip during the process.

Making Tubing

Some people prefer to make their own tubing, either for the pleasure of the process or because they need a size or material not readily available. Start with a strip of thin metal slightly wider than three times the intended diameter. To make a 4 mm tube, start with a strip 14 mm wide (3 x 4 mm + some more, in this case 2). It's easy enough to draw a tube down if your guess was a little generous, but impractical to make it larger.

Use sheet metal no thicker than 24-gauge and start by creating a perfectly straight edge along one side of the sheet. Set a pair of dividers to the intended width and pull these along the sheet so one leg runs along the straight edge. The other point will trace a crisp line that is reliably parallel. Saw this out neatly and smooth it with a flat file. I suggest working with strips roughly 3" to 6" long: much shorter, and it's not worth the bother; much longer, and the process can become awkward.

With a saw or snips, cut a point

on one end of the strip. Most of the forming of the tube will be accomplished by the drawplate, but it's necessary to get the curve started first. Set the strip on a piece of rubber or a sandbag or across a trough cut into a block of wood, and lay a solid rod (such as a large nail) along its length. Strike the rod with a mallet, and then tap the strip so it wraps around the mandrel. The goal is not to form the complete tube, but to make a trough that is in cross-section slightly more than a half circle. It's especially important that the pointed end is well shaped because this is where the form first starts to take shape.

As described above, pull the strip through the drawplate with a smooth perpendicular motion. If the point was symmetrical, the seam will probably be straight. If the tube appears to rotate slightly, this will not cause a problem. In the end, the seam will be invisible.

Pull the strip through successively smaller holes until the edges *just* touch. If the gap is not perfectly parallel, insert a strip of sandpaper folded over so it has grit facing out on both sides and pull this along the seam until it travels smoothly. Anneal the strip and pull it through one or two holes—just until the edges touch. Clean the tube with Scotch-Brite (drawplates are often oily or waxy), apply flux, and close the seam with hard solder. After pickling, rinsing and drying, file off any lumps of solder and pull the tube through one or two holes in the drawplate to "erase" the seam. This tube can be used like any other, including additional drawing as needed.

Mariko Kusumoto, *Altar #1,* music box with movement. Sterling, copper, brass, nickel silver, found objects, 10½"H x 6"W x 3"D, photo: M. Lee Fatherree. "Metal has been a familiar material to me since I was a child; polishing the elaborate metal ornaments in the Buddhist temple where my father was a priest was one of my chores. When the gleam of these gold-colored ornaments would emerge from the darkness, I could sense the spiritual world and its eternal silence."

Using Reamers

Reamers are specialized tools used to refine and slightly enlarge the interior of holes and tubing. They are not essential to making hinges, but they give a high level of sophistication for those people who really want to make their hinges perfect. Reamers are slightly tapered rods of hardened tool steel, generally between 4" and 8" long. Each rod is a five-sided shaft, and the regular facets of each tool are carefully cut in such a way that they create sharp edges where the facets meet. This is the cutting edge of this subtle tool.

grace delvalle, *His and Her Jewelboxes.* Copper, brass, glass, 8"H x 3"W x 3"D and 7"H x 4"W x 4"D, photo: G. Post.

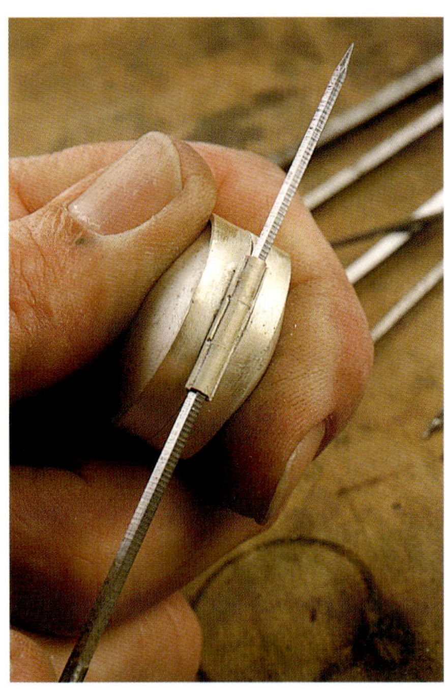

Reamers are used to enlarge holes or to scrape away metal from inside a tube. When making hinges, reamers are used to provide increased friction between the hinge pin and the interior of the knuckles.

Reamers are slid into a tube and rotated back and forth. To make the intended tapered interior, insert from one end only. It's helpful, particularly with the smaller reamers, to mount the tools in a handle. Periodically during use, slide the reamer out and wipe it clean on a rag to remove the almost microscopic shavings of metal being scraped from the inside wall of the tubing. The effect of this process is to create an internal passage for the hinge pin in which the walls are perfectly uniform and slightly conical.

To complete the hinge, file a hinge-pin wire with a subtle taper that matches the taper of the reamer. When this is slid into the hinge, it will make tight contact all along its length. This will hold it into place better and simultaneously make a hinge that has no wobble ("zero play").

Peggy Johnson, *Wok Container With Fish Necklace.* Sterling, 14K, 1 1/4"H x 1"W x 1"D, photo: Michelle Frentrop. This charming and whimsical box contains a necklace with a fish. More than that, the chopsticks double as earrings.

Appendices

Tara Stephenson, *Confidence, Security and Control.* Sterling, Plexiglas mirror, powder puff, 3"H x 2"W x $2^1/_2$"D. (Also shown on page 56.)

Appendix A
Glossary

Abrasives. Natural or man-made grit, either glued onto paper or combined with rubber, ceramic or wax to make tools that shape, smooth and polish metal. Traditional abrasives include sandstone and garnet; modern developments include silicon carbide and aluminum oxide. Grits are designated by mesh size (holes per inch) of sorting screens.

Alloy. A mixture of metals, usually creating a material with improved properties and lower cost. Sterling, for example, is a combination of silver (92.5 percent) and copper that is tougher than either component.

Annealing. The process of heating metal to relieve internal stresses that would otherwise make the metal break, rather than bend. Annealing temperatures differ for each alloy, but are typically around two-thirds of the melting temperature.

Bail. The loop or hook from which a pendant is suspended.

Bench pin. A block of wood that projects out from a jeweler's bench to provide support for filing, sawing and other handworking. Each worker shapes the bench pin to suit individual needs and working styles.

Bezel. In boxes, the band of metal that provides friction to keep a lid closed. The bezel is typically a thin wall on the inside of either the lid or the box. In jewelry, the bezel is a thin wall of metal that surrounds and secures a gem.

Binding wire. Ferrous wire (steel or iron) used to tie parts together during soldering. Wire sold specifically for this purpose is annealed to make it easy to wrap and oxidized to reduce the threat of parts adhering to each other.

Brazing. A method of joining metals at high temperatures. Brazing requires that the metals being joined are heated close to their melting points. Soldering, more correctly called *silver brazing*, allows for joining metals at lower temperatures by using high-silver alloys.

Burnishing. A process of smoothing and polishing metals or other soft materials by rubbing them with a smooth, hard tool. Burnishing is probably the oldest means of polishing silver, copper and gold.

Catch. A mechanical closure on a utilitarian object such as a box.

Clasp. A closure on a wearable item like a necklace or bracelet.

Dapping die. A wooden or steel block with hemispherical depressions of various sizes. In conjunction with "mating" dapping punches, this ancient tool is used to form flat sheet into domes. Dapping punches—strong, blunt rods with a rounded end—are also useful for nonconforming dies and other forming operations.

Depletion gilding. The process of creating a thin skin of a specific metal by leaching away other ingredients in the parent metal. In the case of sterling, for example, copper in the alloy is converted to copper oxide by heating. This is then dissolved in pickle, leaving only silver on the surface of the object.

Drawplate. A tool (typically made of hardened steel) with tapered holes in a range of sizes. When a soft wire is pulled through the plate, it is reduced in diameter and, depending on the shape of the holes, possibly altered in cross-section.

Firescale. An internal "stain" caused when metallic oxides are trapped inside the structure of an alloy. The frequency, tenacity and damage of firescales differs from one alloy to the next. It can occur in several jewelry metals, but the most common references are to sterling.

Flame types. Torch flames are significantly altered by the relative amounts of fuel and oxygen. When the two ingredients are evenly matched, the result is called a *neutral* flame—all available fuel is consumed without an excess of oxygen remaining in the area. A fuel-rich flame is called *reducing* because it reduces the likelihood of oxidation. A flame in which there is not enough fuel to combine with all the oxygen present is called an *oxidizing* flame.

Flux. A chemical used to facilitate soldering by absorbing oxides.

Hinges. Mechanical devices that are solid materials, but allow parts to move as if they were flexible. Hinges can be made in a vast range of sizes and shapes. The most common version uses sections of tube called *knuckles.*

Invisible rivets. Cold connections that are made of the same alloy as the material being joined and countersunk to blend incompletely. Also called "disappearing rivets."

Knuckles. The individual parts that make up a hinge. Knuckles are conventionally grouped in odd numbers (3, 5, 7, etc.) with the larger number attached to the larger piece (either body or lid).

Layout. The process (and result) of transferring a design onto a workpiece. Care in layout is the first step in construction.

Mallets. Hammer-like tools made of wood, leather, plastic or other nonmetal materials that will not radically alter the thickness of a sheet when struck.

Pickle. A strong chemical used to dissolve oxides and other scale from metal. Proprietary compounds are used today, but their predecessors were vinegar and other naturally occurring organic mixtures.

Planishing. The process of using a polished hammer to refine and polish a metal surface.

Rivets. Lengths of rod used to form a mechanical connection between parts. Rivets can be purchased or made from pieces of wire that have been hammered to create a thickened head on both ends. In addition to basic versions, there are a number of creative variations including "invisible rivets," "tube rivets" and "ornamental rivets."

Rebecca Reimers Cristol, *Ammonite Box.* Sterling, fossil ammonite, 2"H x 2$^{1}/_{8}$"W x 1$^{1}/_{16}$"D, photo: Dixon Withers-Julian. The box was constructed from textured sheet and the element on which the fossil sits was cast.

Sanding sticks. Strips of wood or plastic used as backing for abrasive papers. Commercial versions are sold through jewelry supply companies; flat pieces of wood about the size of a ruler are typical.

Scoring. The process of cutting a V-shaped groove into metal to allow it to make a sharp bend. Scoring is done with files, gravers, scrapers, or milling equipment, or by stamping.

Soldering investment. A plaster-like white powder that is used to hold parts in alignment for soldering.

Tabs. Small panels of metal that are bent over to mechanically hold parts, either permanently or as a temporary measure, while other means like solder or glue are used.

Wire soldering. The process of feeding solder that has been manufactured into the shape of wire. Typically this process is used to supply metal into a seam with maximum efficiency.

Work hardening. The process of developing stress in a piece of metal by partially exhausting its malleability. Work hardening might be a negative quality, as when more forming needs to be done. It can also be positive, as when it makes a piece less likely to bend out of shape during use.

Appendix B

Suppliers

General Tools And Materials

Allcraft Tool and Supply
666 Pacific Street
Brooklyn, NY 11217
(800) 645-7124
(212) 840-1860
(718) 253-0443 Fax

Armstrong Tool and Supply
31747 West 8 Mile Road
Livonia, MI 48152
(800) 446-9694
(248) 474-1600

Jules Borel and Co.
1110 Grand Boulevard
Kansas City, MO 64106
(800) 333-4646
(816) 421-6110
(816) 421-2596 Fax

E.B. Fitler and Co.
RD2, Box 176B
Milton, DE 19968
(800) 346-2497
(302) 684-1893 Fax

Forslev's
210 South Milwaukee
Wheeling, IL 60090
(847) 520-4120
(847) 520-4437 Fax

Frei and Borel
126 2nd Street
PO Box 796
Oakland, CA 94604
(800) 772-3456
(415) 832-0355
(415) 834-6217 Fax

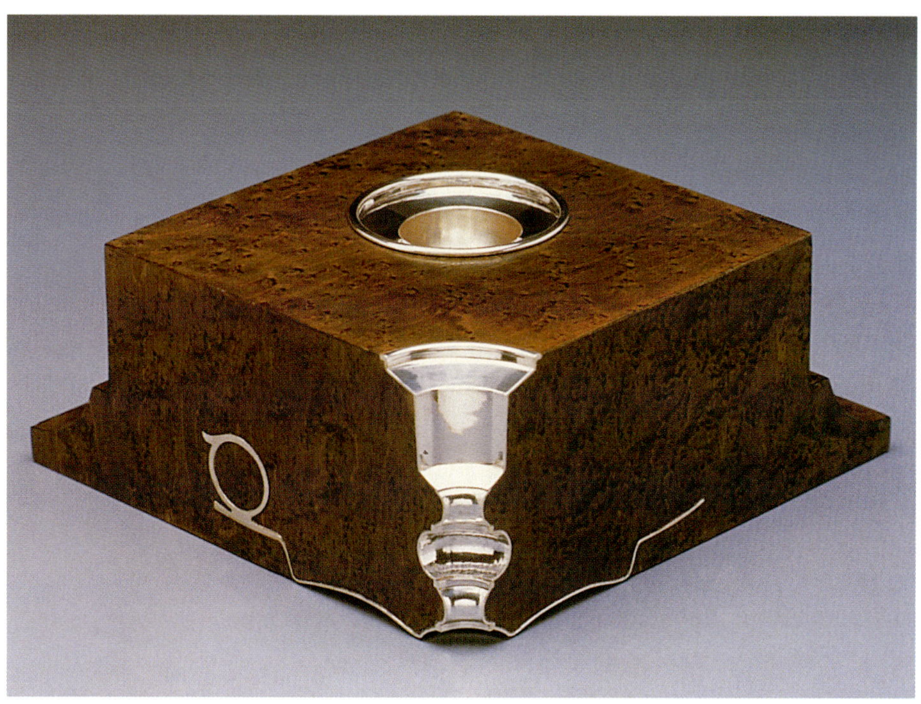

Myra Mimlitsch Gray, *Candleholder II*. Sterling, brass, bird's eye maple veneer, 7$^{1}/_{4}$"H x 7$^{1}/_{4}$"W x 3$^{1}/_{4}$"D.

Gesswein
255 Hancock Avenue
Bridgeport, CA 06605
(800) 243-4466
(203) 366-5400
(203) 366-3953 Fax

T.B. Hagstoz and Son
709 Sansom Street
Philadelphia, PA 19106
(215) 922-1627
(215) 922-7126 Fax

C.R. Hill Co.
2734 West 11 Mile Road
Berkley, MI 48072
(800) 521-1221
(248) 543-9104 Fax

Rio Grande
7500 Bluewater Road NW
Albuquerque, NM 87121-1962
(800) 545-6566
(800) 965-2329 Fax

C.W. Somers Co.
373 Washington Street
Boston, MA 02108
(800) 322-1003
(617) 426-6880

Swest Inc.
11090 North Stemmons Frwy.
Dallas, TX 75229
(800) 527-5057
(972) 247-7744
(972) 247-3507 Fax

TSI, Inc.
101 Nickerson Street
Seattle, WA 98109
(800) 426-9984
(206) 282-3040
(206) 281-8701 Fax

William Dixon Co.
750 Washington Avenue
Carlstadt, NJ 07072
(800) 847-4188
(201) 935-0100

Metals

Admiral Metals
11 Forbes Road
Woburn, MA 01801
(800) 423-6472
(781) 933-8300

Centaur Forge
117 North Spring Street
Burlington, WI 53105
(800) 666-9175
(414) 763-9175
(414) 763-8350 Fax

Hauser Miller
PO Box 500700
10950 Lynvalle Road
St. Louis, MO 63123
(800) 462-7447
(314) 487-1311

Hoover and Strong
10700 Trade Road
Richmond, VA 23236
(800) 759-9997
(804) 794-3700
(804) 794-5687 Fax

Tara Peck, box. Brass, 2" cube, photos: Mark Johnston.

Miscellaneous

Bryant Labs, Inc.
Patina Chemicals
1101 Fifth Street
Berkeley, CA 94710
(800) 367-3141
(510) 526-3141
(510) 528-2948 Fax

Griffith's Distributors
Flux
PO Box 662
Louisville, CO 80027
(303) 442-8284
(303) 665-5108 Fax

J.I. Morris Co.
Small Screws
394 Elm Street
Southbridge, MA 01550
(508) 764-4394
(508) 764-7350 Fax

Reactive Metals Studio
Niobium, Equipment, Findings
PO Box 890
Clarksdale, AZ 86324
(800) 876-3434
(520) 634-3434

Small Parts

Equipment and Supplies
13980 NW 58 Court
PO Box 4650
Miami Lakes, FL 33014-0650
(800) 220-4242
(305) 751-0856

Appendix C

Suggested Reading

Coloring, Bronzing and Patination of Metals
Hughes and Rowe
Watson-Guptill, New York, NY
1982

The Complete Metalsmith
Tim McCreight
Davis Publications, Worcester, MA
1991

Design and Creation of Jewelry
Robert von Neumann
Chilton Publishers, Radnor, PA
1989

Hinges and Hinge-Based Catches for Jewelers and Goldsmiths
Charles Lewton-Brain
Brain Press, Calgary, Alberta, Canada
1997

Hydraulic Die Forming for Jewelers and Metalsmiths
Susan Kingsley
20-Ton Press, Carmel, CA
1993

Jewelry: Contemporary Design and Technique
Chuck Evans
Davis Publications, Worcester, MA
1989

Jewelry: Fundamentals of Metalsmithing
Tim McCreight
Hand Books Press, Madison, WI
1997

Metal Techniques for Craftsmen
Oppi Untracht
Doubleday, New York, NY
1968

Practical Casting
Tim McCreight
Brynmorgen Press, Portland, Maine
1986, revised 1994

Silver Boxes
Eric Delieb
Clarkson N. Potter, Inc. New York, NY
1968

Appendix D

Tables & Charts

TEMPERATURE COMPARISONS

To convert Centigrade to Fahrenheit:
—Multiply degrees C by 9.
—Divide by 5.
—Add 32.

°C	°F	°C	°F
0	32	650	1202
50	122	675	1247
75	167	700	1292
100	212	725	1337
125	257	750	1382
150	302	775	1427
175	347	800	1472
200	392	825	1517
225	437	850	1562
250	482	875	1607
275	527	900	1652
300	572	925	1697
325	617	950	1742
350	662	975	1787
375	707	1000	1832
400	752	1025	1877
425	797	1050	1922
450	842	1075	1967
475	887	1100	2012
500	932	1125	2057
525	977	1150	2102
550	1022	1175	2147
575	1067	1200	2192
600	1112	1225	2237
625	1157	1250	2282

To convert Fahrenheit to Centigrade:
—Subtract 32 from degrees F.
—Multiply by 5.
—Divide by 9.

°F	°C	°F	°C
32	0	1300	704
100	38	1350	732
150	66	1400	760
200	93	1450	788
250	121	1500	816
300	149	1550	843
350	177	1600	871
400	204	1650	899
450	232	1700	927
500	260	1750	954
550	288	1800	982
600	316	1850	1010
650	343	1900	1038
700	371	1950	1066
750	399	2000	1093
800	427	2050	1121
850	454	2100	1149
900	482	2150	1177
950	510	2200	1204
1000	538	2250	1232
1050	566	2300	1260
1100	593	2350	1288
1150	621	2400	1316
1200	649	2450	1343
1250	677	2500	1371

ALLOYS

symbol		Au	Ag	Cu	Zn	other	melting point °C	melting point °F	specific gravity
Al	Aluminum					100 Al	660	1220	2.7
Sb	Antimony					100 Sb	631	1168	6.6
Bi	Bismuth					100 Bi	271	520	9.8
260	Brass, cartridge			70	30		954	1749	8.5
226	Jewelers Bronze			88	12		1030	1886	8.7
220	Red Brass			90	10		1044	1910	8.8
511	Bronze			96		4 Sn	1060	1945	8.8
Cd	Cadmium					100 Cd	321	610	8.7
Cr	Chromium					100 Cr	1890	3434	6.9
Cu	Copper			100			1083	1981	8.9
Au	Gold (fine)	100					1063	1945	19.3
920	22K Yellow	92	4	4			977	1790	17.3
900	22K Coinage	90	10				940	1724	17.2
750	18K Yellow	75	15	10			882	1620	15.5
750	18K Yellow	75	12.5	12.5			904	1660	15.5
750	18K Green	75	25				966	1770	15.6
750	18K Rose	75	5	20			932	1710	15.5
750	18K White	75				25 Pd	904	1660	15.7
580	14K Yellow	58	25	17			802	1476	13.4
580	14K Green	58	35	7			835	1534	13.6
580	14K Rose	58	10	32			827	1520	13.4
580	14K White	58				42 Pd	927	1700	13.7
420	10K Yellow	42	12	41	5		786	1447	11.6
420	10K Yellow	42	7	48	3		876	1609	11.6
420	10K Green	42	58				804	1480	11.7
420	10K Rose	42	10	48			810	1490	11.6
420	10K White	42				58 Pd	927	1760	11.8
Fe	Iron					100 Fe	1535	2793	7.9
Pb	Lead					100 Pb	327	621	11.3
Mg	Magnesium					100 Mg	651	1204	1.7
	Monel Metals			33		60 Ni, 7 Fe	1360	2480	8.9
Ni	Nickel					100 Ni	1455	2651	8.8
752	Nickel Silver			65	17	18 Ni	1110	2030	8.8
Pd	Palladium					100 Pd	1549	2820	12.2
	Old Pewter					80 Pb, 20 Sn	304	580	9.5
Pt	Platinum					100 Pt	1774	3225	21.4
Ag	Silver (fine)		100				961	1762	10.6
925	Sterling		92.5	7.5			920	1640	10.4
800	Coin Silver		80	20			890	1634	10.3
	Mild Steel					99 Fe, 1 C	1511	2750	7.9
	Stainless Steel					91 Fe, 9 Cr	1371	2500	7.8
Sn	Tin					100 Sn	232	450	7.3
Ti	Titanium					100 Ti	1800	3272	4.5
Zn	Zinc				100		419	786	7.1

WEIGHT PER SQUARE INCH OF SHEET

mm	inch	B&S	fine silver OUNCES	sterling OUNCES	fine gold DWTS. *	10K DWTS.	14K DWTS.	18K DWTS.	platinum OUNCES
6.54	.2576	2	1.42	1.41	52.5	31.4	35.5	42.3	2.91
5.19	.2043	4	1.12	1.12	41.6	24.9	28.1	33.6	2.31
4.11	.1620	6	.894	.884	33.0	19.8	22.3	26.6	1.83
3.26	.1285	8	.709	.701	26.2	15.7	17.7	21.1	1.45
2.59	.1019	10	.562	.556	20.8	12.4	14.0	16.7	1.15
2.05	.0808	12	.446	.441	16.5	9.85	11.1	13.3	.913
1.63	.0641	14	.354	.350	13.1	7.81	8.82	10.5	.724
1.29	.0508	16	.281	.277	10.4	6.21	7.00	8.35	.574
1.02	.0403	18	.223	.220	8.20	4.91	5.55	6.62	.455
.813	.0320	20	.176	.174	6.51	3.90	4.40	5.25	.361
.643	.0253	22	.140	.138	5.16	3.09	3.49	4.216	.286
.511	.0201	24	.111	.110	4.09	2.45	2.77	3.30	.227
.404	.0154	26	.088	.087	3.24	1.94	2.19	2.62	.180
.330	.0126	28	.070	.069	2.58	1.54	1.74	2.08	.143
.254	.0100	30	.055	.055	2.04	1.22	1.38	1.65	.113

WEIGHT PER FOOT OF WIRE

mm	inch	B&S	fine silver OUNCES	sterling OUNCES	fine gold DWTS. *	10K DWTS.	14K DWTS.	18K DWTS.	platinum OUNCES
6.54	.2576	2	3.45	3.41	128	76.3	86.1	104	7.07
5.19	.2043	4	2.17	2.14	80.1	48.0	54.2	64.6	4.45
4.11	.1620	6	1.36	1.35	50.4	30.2	34.1	40.6	2.80
3.26	.1285	8	.856	.848	31.6	19.0	21.4	25.6	1.76
2.59	.1019	10	.541	.534	20.0	11.9	13.5	16.1	1.11
2.05	.0808	12	.339	.335	12.6	7.50	8.47	10.1	.695
1.63	.0641	14	.214	.211	7.87	4.72	5.33	6.36	.437
1.29	.0508	16	.135	.132	4.96	2.97	3.35	4.00	.275
1.02	.0403	18	.085	.084	3.11	1.87	2.11	2.51	.173
.813	.0320	20	.053	.053	1.96	1.17	1.33	1.58	.109
.643	.0253	22	.034	.033	1.28	.738	.833	.994	.068
.511	.0201	24	.021	.021	.775	.464	.524	.625	.043
.404	.0154	26	.013	.013	.488	.292	.330	.393	.027
.330	.0126	28	.008	.008	.306	.184	.287	.247	.017
.254	.0100	30	.005	.005	.193	.115	.130	.155	.010

* DWTS. = pennyweights

RELATIVE SIZES & WEIGHTS

To find the weight of a given object if it were made in a different metal, multiply by the factors shown. For instance, if I have a sterling ring that weighs 6 dwts. (known) and I want to know its weight in 18K yellow gold (query), 6 x 1.48 = 8.8 dwts. (pennyweights).

Query	Known	Factor
18KY (yellow) Gold	18KW (white)	1.064
	platinum	.723
	brass	1.885
	sterling	1.480
14KY Gold	18KW	.842
	14KW	1.035
	platinum	.609
	brass	1.589
	sterling	1.248
10KY Gold	18 KY	.745
	14 KW	.884
	platinum	.539
	brass	1.406
	sterling	1.104
Platinum	palladium	1.758
	iridium	.953
	10% irid plat	.995
	15% irid plat	.993
	rhodium	1.717
	ruthenium	1.771
	sterling	2.046
Sterling	fine silver	.984
	coin silver	1.004
	18KY	.675
	14KY	.801
	10KY	.905
	platinum	.488
	brass	1.273

RELATIVE SIZES & WEIGHTS

B&S	mm	inches thousandths/fractions		drill size
0	8.5	.325	21/64	
1	7.35	.289	9/32	
2	6.54	.258	1/4	
3	5.83	.229	7/32	1
4	5.19	.204	13/64	6
5	4.62	.182	3/16	15
6	4.11	.162	5/32	20
7	3.67	.144	9/64	27
8	3.26	.129	1/8	30
10	2.59	.102		38
11	2.30	.090	3/32	43
12	2.05	.080	5/64	46
13	1.83	.072		50
14	1.63	.064	1/16	51
15	1.45	.057		52
16	1.29	.050		54
17	1.15	.045	3/64	55
18	1.02	.040		56
19	.912	.036		60
20	.813	.032	1/32	65
21	.724	.029		67
22	.643	.025		70
23	.574	.023		71
24	.511	.020		74
25	.455	.018		75
26	.404	.016	1/64	77
27	.361	.014		78
28	.330	.013		79
29	.279	.011		80
30	.254	.010		

Appendix E

Contributing Artists

Abrasha
San Francisco, California–page 33

Rachel Alvarez
Portland, Maine–pages 64, 80, 85

Talya Baharal
Rifton, New York–pages 7, 9, 20

Jan Baum
Portland, Oregon–front cover, 36, 59

Lilyana Bekic
Berwyn, Illinois–page 78

Susan Bickford
Yarmouth, Maine–page 46

Teri Blond
San Antonio, Texas–page 118

Patricia Bolz
Camden, Maine–pages 5, 111

Elizabeth Bone
London, England–page 87

Kathleen Browne
Ravenna, Ohio–page 109

Jane Campbell
Cambridge Springs, Pennsylvania–pages 96, 97

Tina Chisena
Wheaton, Maryland–page 41

Adam "Monkey Shines" Clark
San Francisco, California–page 35

Ken Cory
(deceased) pages 88, 125, 141

Rebecca Reimers Cristol
Williamsburg, Virginia–page 133

J. Cummings
Heltonville, Indiana–page 51

Nancy Deal
Seattle, Washington–page 114

Ken Cory, *Window Box.* Copper, sterling, enamel, glass, spectrolite, 2 5/8"H x 1 1/4"W x 1 1/4"D, photo: Lynn Thompson.

grace delvalle
Larkspur, California–page 128

Nicole DesChamps
Ann Arbor, Michigan–page 2

Tara Etheridge
Ames, Iowa–page 45

Chuck Evans
Ames, Iowa–page 19

Martha A. Feldhaus
Grants Pass, Oregon–page 93

Richard Finney
Winnipeg, Manitoba, Canada–page 39

Ned Foulkrod
Boothwyn, Pennsylvania–page 66

Dominique Giordano
New Orleans, Louisiana–page 84

Gabrielle Gould
St. Augustine, Florida–page 143

Lee Graham
Albeshot, England–page 61

John J. Grant
Santa Monica, California–page 12

Myra Mimlitsch Gray
Stone Ridge, New York–page 134

Bobby Hansson
Rising Sun, Maryland–page 100

Jan Harrell
Houston, Texas–page 75

Kathy Hart
Worcester, Massachusetts–page 121

Caryn L. Hetherston
Landenberg, Pennsylvania–page 113

Chris Irick
Dallas, Texas–pages 52, 63, 73, 98, 115

Peggy Johnson
Portland, Maine–page 129

Tracy Johnson
Brunswick, Maine–page 86

David Jones
Saluda, North Carolina–pages 38, 70, 72, 123

Kristina Kada
Felton, California–pages 7, 18, 26, 109

Joana Kao
Seattle, Washington–page 44

Deborah Krupenia
Waltham, Massachusetts–front cover, 16

Mariko Kusumoto
San Francisco, California–pages 21, 47, 55, 108, 127

Debbie LaFara
St. Louis, Missouri–page 52

Elise Landry
Boone, North Carolina–page 43

Lorraine Lenskold
Chatham, New Jersey–pages 40, 121

Micki Lippe
Seattle, Washington–pages 13, 25, 124, 126

Marcia A. Macdonald
Eugene, Oregon–page 24

Merideth Malony
Ballard, West Virginia–page 25

Jane Martin
Bainbridge Island, Washington–page 22

Jiro J. Masuda
Royal Oaks, Michigan–page 48

Tim McCreight
Portland, Maine–pages 11, 21

Jason Morrissey
Portland, Maine–page 107

Joe Muench
St. Louis, Missouri–page 105

Thomas P. Muir
Perrysburg, Ohio–page 68

Steve A. Musselman
Carbondale, Illinois–pages 27, 53

Dan Natkiel
New York City, New York–page 95

j.e. Paterak
Portland, Maine–page 91

Tara Peck
Somerville, Massachusetts–page 135

Alan Perry
Portsmouth, New Hampshire–pages 42, 81

Frances J. Pickens
Honolulu, Hawaii–pages 40, 126

Suzanne Pugh
Brooklyn, New York–page 42

Jon Michael Route
Frederic, Wisconsin–pages 17, 124

Glenda Rowley
page 112

Addison Saunders
Ellsworth, Maine–page 121

Jennifer Schellenbach
Fruita, Colorado–page 15

Marjorie Simon
Highland Park, New Jersey–page 6

Kiff Slemmons
Seattle, Washington–front cover, 10, 99

Albion Smith
Santa Cruz, California–pages 31, 125

Mark Stanitz
Rochester, New York–page 8

Tara Stephenson
Bowling Green, Ohio–pages 30, 49, 56, 131

Lori Talcott
Seattle, Washington–front cover, 3, 67

Carol Webb
Santa Cruz, California–front cover, 37

Mary Schimpff Webb
New Smyrna Beach, Florida–pages 116, 117

Ken Weston
Hillsborough, North Carolina–page 23

Brent Williams
Portland, Maine–pages 54, 101, 119

Kat Winters
Hamilton, Ohio–page 57

Jeff Wise
Durango, Colorado–page 83

Cappy Counard Wolf
Murphysboro, Illinois–pages 76, 77

Paula Wolfe
Marlborough, Massachusetts–page 102

Kee-Ho Yuen
Cedar Falls, Iowa–page 110

Stephen Yusko
Makanda, Illinois–back cover, 122

Index

Gabrielle Gould, *Bird on a Cloud,* locket pendant. Sterling, 14K, feather, $2^1/_2$"H x $3^1/_2$"W x $^5/_8$"D.